Endorsements

"God has given Joyce an unusual gift for ministering to the specific needs of women through her weekly radio broadcast, *Rejoicing with Joyce International*. Joyce has lovingly written from a practical view. In her book, she ministers to widows as she relates her personal experience of grief and her determination to know and continue to do God's will."

- Dr. and Mrs. James Kennard
International Director, BIMI

"Good Grief—I Need Relief! is a practical book filled with ideas and survival tips from widows who have found joy again. Joyce Webster candidly shares how she journaled when her missionary husband died in a foreign country. She also encourages widows to find comfort in God's Word. This book helps widows realize that we all share much of the same valley of grief. It brings hope to any widow who wants to progress in her journey."

- Karen Kalapp,
widowed missionary

"Good Grief—I Need Relief! is a potpourri of hope, inspiration, comfort, and practical tips for widows. Blossoming from this mix will come a family heirloom of life and love, a treasure for the reader as she fills out the well-guided reflections integrated into each chapter.

Joyce draws from almost fifty years of marriage, plus

church, Christian radio, and missionary work, to give widows a healthy and effective outlet for their grief. It's as if two friends, the author and the reader, are talking together about the things in life that really matter for eternity. This book can also be used as a reference of biblical comfort for pastors, counselors, and grief group facilitators."

- Ferree Hardy,
author of *Postcards from the Widows' Path,*
and blogger at www.WidowsChristianPlace.com

"I have known Joyce and her deceased husband, Warren, for over thirty-five years. As pastor of their sending church, I've had much interest in their work in Japan. Joyce has written a book that will be a great help to so many widows going through the ups and downs of sorrow and loss.

I have been very impressed with the practicality of this book. It is a book that will instruct each grieving person with truths in dealing with sorrow, as only one who has lived it can communicate."

- Dr. John Paisley,
Senior Pastor,
Riverview Baptist Church, Pasco, Washington

"Becoming a widow is one of life's most dreaded circumstances. When this tragedy occurs, ladies are desperate for help. Joyce Webster's book *Good Grief—I Need Relief!* is a book that will help widows. Also, Christian workers can refer to it time and again to help those sorrowing.

Joyce lives the principles she teaches in the book. She is always looking for ways to be a blessing to others. I can sincerely say I have seen Jesus in her! When you read this book, you will be visiting with a lady who knows how to take her woes to the Lord and let Him take control."

- **Becky Patterson**,
wife of Dr. Mike Patterson,
Veteran missionaries to Mexico

"Good Grief—I Need Relief! will bring comfort to widows in knowing that someone else has traveled the path they are going down. It will be a huge help and blessing for those "in grief and wanting relief"!

- **CindieTrieber**,
author of *With All My Heart*,
and Pastor's wife of Dr. Jack Trieber
North Valley Baptist Church, Santa Clara, California

Good Grief— I Need Relief!

A Widow's Guide to Recovering and Rejoicing

Joyce Webster

A Gift for You

_____

From:

_____

Date:

_____

A note to let you know:

_____

_____

_____

As the Lord holds you in His hands,
May the fragrance of His beauty
As the sweetness of a rose,
Bless you and envelop your friends and family.

Good Grief—I Need Relief! A Widow's Guide to Recovering and Rejoicing

© 2016 by Joyce Webster

Printed in the United States of America by Comfort Press.

ISBN: 978-0996529303

Scripture quotations are taken from the King James Bible.

Editor: Elizabeth Honeycutt
Cover Design: Delia Dobbs
Interior Design: Amber Smart

At the time of publication, internet addresses, email addresses, and phone numbers in this book were accurate. They are provided as a resource, and all content may not be endorsed or the permanence guaranteed by this author.

This book contains personal experiences; it is not to be considered medical advice.

Dedication

To my beautiful, sweet mother, Susie Dobbs Bowen. Thank you for supporting my writing without complaining. God bless you, mom, for your encouraging words and for being a great Christian example of a widow twice over. I love you dearly.

Acknowledgements

Thank you, Jim Hills, for reigniting a love for writing in me, and pushing me to attend the writing conference that changed my life. David Sanford, your classes on publishing and personal encouragement made this book happen. I am grateful to both of you for believing in me when I didn't.

A Christian writer always needs friends to hold up their hands when they feel faint. I had such a prayer team; I thank you so much for your wonderful support. God bless each of you for lifting my needs up to the throne: Wanda Brittain, Glenn and Delia Dobbs, Dona Erquiaga, Tammy Garza, Sherry Griffin, Mindy Hyberg, Carol Keister, Haruna McKittrick, Barbara Morse, and Jeanne Williams.

Bless you, Elizabeth Honeycutt, for your expert editing of my manuscript. I know it was a monumental task, which you handled adeptly.

Amber Smart, you came with high recommendations and lived up to them with your interior design. Many thanks.

Delia Dobbs, my sister-in-law and the sister I never had, thank you for your hard work on the cover and your professional advice in the different stages of the book. I couldn't have made it without you.

I am grateful for your sage advice, my brother,

advisor, and confidant, Glenn Dobbs. Thank you for rejoicing with me over small and major milestones, and for letting me interrupt your life so many times when I needed you. You and Delia are the greatest!

Contents

Part Three: LOOKING FORWARD

Part Four: LOOKING UP

INTRODUCTION

*D*ear Widowed Friend,

May I call you friend, since we share the same status?

I wish we could sit together in a quiet spot in a flowering garden and share a cup of tea or coffee and some sweets. I would look you in the eye and say, "Tell me your story." Since we can't, shall we share some sweet thoughts throughout this book instead?

Please feel free to follow the format of this book and answer the questions at the end of each chapter in the spaces provided; or write them in your own journal. It will help you move forward.

Who Should Journal?

- All widows

- All widowers

- Anyone who wants to share their stories

Why Should You Journal?

How much do you know about your grandparents, great grandparents or further back?

- Maybe you have a picture, but do you know what they did for a living?

- What they enjoyed doing in their leisure time?

- Were they Christians?

- How and where did they meet their mates?

Journaling isn't the same as writing a novel or a non-fiction book, and it doesn't require attending a special class. It's simply telling your husband's and your life's stories to leave a legacy for coming generations so they will know some unique facts about you—and not just view your pictures.

"That the generation to come might know them, even the children which should be born; who should arise and declare them to their children: that they might set their hope in God, and not forget the works of God, but keep his commandments: and might not be as their fathers, a stubborn and rebellious generation; a generation that set not their heart aright, and whose spirit was not steadfast with God" (Ps. 78:6-8).

Who Will Write Your Story?

Obviously you are the only one who can determine what your story will contain. As you write your thoughts and reactions down, your different senses can trigger memories, even forgotten moments that mean a lot to complete and enhance your story. You can write it yourself, tell it to someone who can write if for you, video or audio record it, but get it down before the color fades from vivid to pastel to gray.

Is There an Easy Way To Journal?

Yes, I can help! You have a chance to share your stories by answering the questions at the end of each chapter in this book. However, if you use the companion journal book along with this book, you will have several more comprehensive questions to help you better add specific details to make your situation come alive. If you don't write your story, all your life's memories die with you.

- Most people don't.

- Most people won't.

- Will you be the exception?

Bless your heritage by sharing family stories and traditions; they deserve it.

Growing through Journaling

As we journal together in this book, may we grow through our anger, depression, frustrations, inexpressible fears, and tears, to see our down-days flipped over like a calendar, into up-days.

Why did God choose our beloved, our buffer zone, our comforter, our companion, confidant, safety net, and security to live with Him, and choose for us to remain here?

Simply put, we have an unfulfilled purpose, or maybe more than one.

- Perhaps that purpose is to leave a family legacy through our journal, which shows the way the Lord provided for our needs during our married life and in widowhood.

- Possibly it's to care for an aging parent, as was my case.

- Does the Lord want to use you to write your story to share with others outside your family?

- Maybe it's to gain more knowledge so we can touch an audience as we stand before them to teach, speak, or to reach out to an unseen online presence and encourage their lives.

- Our neighborhood just might need our godly influence as they see us wade through deep, troubled waters and come out in the sunshine.

- If nothing else, maybe it's to grasp the inner peace for which all are searching.

- Or perhaps it's something unrevealed at this time.

God doesn't owe us a reason for what He does. If He gave us one, it still wouldn't return our husband. However, we don't have to grieve alone. He has promised never to leave us nor forsake us (Heb. 13:5b).

In the past: In the biblical book of Job, how did Job's friends try to console him? They waited quietly without saying a word. Then they took turns talking. So let's try it with a little different twist. I wrote; you read; then you write (silent talking). You can also contact me through my website or Facebook page. The details are listed at the end of the book.

In the present: My prayer for you is that whatever your circumstances, you will accept your new purpose. Taking baby steps each day moves you forward. Even if your faith is small, I trust you have lots of hope (Ps. 71:14a, "But I will hope continually..."), and that hope turns into joy, and then peace blooms again in your heart.

In the future: Be assured He will guide your footsteps. May your future generations get to know you and your husband more intimately through your writing as they read the descriptions of your personalities, quirks, and happy, interesting tidbits. You may also want to add a couple of not-so-good instances, which you will see that I have shared. And may your family gain an understanding of what you went through in your grieving process and how you coped with different issues that arose.

May we heal and rejoice together through the ideas on the following pages.

"He healeth the broken in heart, and bindeth up their wounds" (Ps. 147:3).

Welcome to *Good Grief—I Need Relief! A Widow's Guide to Recovering and Rejoicing.*

Loving Blessings from Your Widowed Friend,

Joyce Webster

Part One

Looking Back

"The memory of the just is blessed…"

(Prov. 10:7a).

Chapter One

∽ A BLEAK DAY ∽
THE FUNERAL

$\mathcal{M}$y missionary husband died unexpectedly in Tokyo, Japan, of a massive heart attack.

I ran across the narrow street and pounded on my neighbor's door. "Help, please help me! My husband isn't breathing!" My American, English-speaking neighbor quickly followed me into my home and began CPR.

"Dial 119! (The emergency code in Japan) Ask them to send an ambulance!"

I dialed. "This is an emergency! Please send an ambulance, my husband isn't breathing. My address is..." Click. Apparently he couldn't understand my English. It mystified me. *Couldn't he tell I was in distress? Why did he hang up? Why didn't he ask a co-worker to help me? Did he even have a co-worker? What now?*

My neighbor grabbed the phone, dialed, and quickly explained our dire circumstances in Japanese. The ambulance arrived shortly, its strange sounding siren alerting the whole neighborhood of our emergency.

Soon, a Japanese neighbor lady knocked on my door while the ambulance lights flashed in the street. She asked, "Would you like for me to ride with you in the ambulance and interpret?" Although I didn't know her well, I replied, "Yes!" We climbed in and sat where the paramedics indicated; her presence eased the strained situation, and made me feel a tad more secure.

I glanced at my unresponsive husband as they continued CPR.

"Please ask them to give him oxygen," I said.

She spoke quickly to the paramedics and then turned and said, "They have given him as much as they can."

Where was I? I must be dreaming. This just can't be real.

I am sure I must have hyperventilated as we rode on and on through the crowded streets. *Why can't we go faster? Why don't people get out of the way? Don't they realize this is an emergency?* The constant whine of the siren throbbed in my head. The ride to the hospital seemed to take forever; in reality it probably lasted about twenty minutes.

News spread quickly and soon some of our church people gathered at the hospital, hugged me, and sat and waited with me. Finally, someone came and announced, "I am sorry, but your husband is dead. We did everything that we could for him."

I didn't scream or cry like I heard some Japanese women do in the distance. It didn't seem to serve a purpose; I felt numb and the whole thing seemed surreal. About three hours after his pain began, the Lord released him from all earthly bonds even though I pleaded, "Oh, God, no! Please don't take him!"

A voice interrupted my thoughts, "We will have him prepared for you to view in a little while."

I nodded.

How and why did this happen?

While still a senior in high school, Warren felt the tug, like a roped calf, to follow his two older brothers into the military; they served as career men, he as a one termer. He loved the regimentation of the military, and the church and people where he now served. Our home welcomed pastors, missionaries, evangelists, family, and military friends. He was a natural fit for the military ministry. Lord, why when everything is going well...?

Another interruption: "Follow me."

I stood with a missionary couple who spoke fluent Japanese and moved into the room where my now deceased husband lay on a gurney. Several Japanese stood in a row at a respectful distance at his feet. Horror grabbed me as I saw his body already discolored to what appeared a mix between a dark purple and a deep red. *Hadn't he just died; how could this happen so soon? The bodies I viewed in funeral homes in the past looked normal. This was anything but normal!*

I stared a few seconds knowing that the men were watching me and wondering just how this American lady would react. I remained calm and said something like, "I know where he is now. He is in heaven with the Lord that he loved. Thank you for caring for him." I bowed the customary way and they returned it. We turned and walked out.

A church lady and I returned to my empty house. After receiving and placing many phone calls, we each chose a couch and lay down to rest for the night. The phone rang at four a.m. A man's voice I recognized said, "I just heard. Please tell me it isn't so!" I had to reply, "You heard right; he is gone."

After I talked to family members, I continued to receive email after email from friends in different sections of the world encouraging me by saying, "I can't believe your husband is dead; you are in our prayers."

The next issue? Looking for a coffin. How and where could I do that? I didn't speak Japanese. Japan, with more population than land, cremates their dead, so there were various hoops to jump through to find one. A friend found pictures online of the three choices I had and emailed them to me. As a whole, the Japanese people are small in stature, so if Warren had been a couple of inches taller, I would have had a real problem finding a coffin long enough. The shape of the one I chose resembled a mummy, the top didn't hinge, and it had a viewing glass. We draped an American flag over the top, and it worked fine.

When funeral arrangements had finalized through my mission board, I went by myself door to door and invited my neighbors to attend the service. All but one family came, and they sent a bouquet of flowers with regrets that they had a previous commitment.

At the church, the ones who graciously took charge (as I had no family in Japan) asked if I would like to say something at the end of the service. I hadn't considered it because time and happenings blurred my brain and sound reasoning flew out the window. However, I said yes and jotted down some thoughts right before the service began. Since our ministry focused mostly on the U.S. military people serving in Japan, it resonated when the Lord impressed me with two words, *"Mission Accomplished!"* Those words encouraged not only the attendees, but also me, to keep living for the Lord until our own *"Mission Accomplished"* date.

American and Japanese neighbors, church folks, and several missionaries from Okinawa and mainland Japan packed the church building and everyone listened attentively as the gospel was presented through songs and preaching. A planned surprise ending included a recording of my husband singing.

One thing redeemed the whole process: the young daughter of a military couple accepted the Lord as her Savior! Heaven smiled.

After the funeral, we gathered upstairs and had our last meal together. The Lord gave me amazing endurance and grace so I could greet everyone with clarity and joy.

Several ladies from the church kindly helped me pack, and took me to the airport about two hours away. We hugged, cried, and prayed together. I was assured that someone would meet me at the airport when I returned to pack my home.

When Warren's body arrived in Pasco, Washington, I had the whole casket ordeal to go through again since I chose the cheapest one in Japan with the thought of replacing it stateside. My pastor graciously showed me the one that he had chosen for his wife, just a couple months prior. Doves flying upward graced the white, satin lining, symbolizing the releasing of the spirit. I liked it immediately.

Easter morning, seven days after Warren died, found my mom, my daughters, and their husbands leaving the motel room to attend church with me. I rolled my extra heavy carry-on bag to the open door of our room, and when it hit the threshold, it fell backward with great force on my right foot. It immediately swelled to the size of a portabella mushroom. I screamed and hopped across the room and lay down on the bed. They applied ice to it and then took me to a critical care clinic. Although X-rays didn't show any broken bones, the pain made it feel like there were several.

When Brother James Kennard, the military director for our mission board (Baptist International Missions Incorporated), saw the condition of my foot, he said he would try to upgrade me to business class to fly back to Japan. That way I would have room to stretch my leg out and take better care of my foot. I felt honored when four people responded and said they would donate air miles to help me upgrade. However, one couple in Japan covered the entire difference.

Later that afternoon, I rolled into the church in a wheelchair for the viewing.

A family friend, Robbie Hiner, recorded "Serenaded by Angels up To the Throne," and sent it special delivery to the church. It arrived in time for the memorial service.

My children Pam, Michelle, and Jonathan sang together, while my other son David played the piano, and his wife, Charise, played the organ. They blessed my heart.

Other people's hearts were touched when Brother James Kennard set a pair of Warren's shoes on the pulpit at the moment he said, "Who will fill Warren's shoes?"

Friends and family joined us at Warren's military graveside ceremony. The veterans ended the service with a gun salute, an impressive flag folding ceremony, and the traditional playing of "Taps."

Our church family graciously provided a meal in the church gymnasium for everyone, allowing us to talk to our extended family surrounded by the warmth of caring friends.

I chose a burial plot that allowed for a double depth burial. Since the government has strict rules about what is allowed on tombstones, my side of the stone is inscribed with his life's verse. It reads: "For me to live is Christ, and to die is gain" (Phil. 1:21).

For some reason, I didn't have the correct discharge papers that were needed by the government so they would pay for his marker. Later I learned his military records had burned in a fire several years prior, and I battled to prove Warren actively served four years in the Air Force with top security clearance. Several months later, things fell into place and finalized.

A couple of weeks after the funeral, when jet lag finally departed and my foot proved up to traveling, I boarded an airplane by myself and returned to Japan to finish the details of packing, selling the cars, taking care of paperwork such as death certificates in a foreign land, and having friends who spoke Japanese work out the details for a container to bring our goods back to the States. I lived with friends on the military base while things finalized, all in the Lord's timing of about a month.

I had the privilege of several church friends helping pack our things for me. A customs list lengthened as the boxes mounted in the living room, each one carefully numbered. People worked behind the scenes to find a container to move everything back to the States. At the same time, people fixed meals for me in their homes or took me on base to eat. A couple of ladies took me shopping out of town. We rode the trains and enjoyed the day watching porpoises perform their aquatic tricks, in spite of the wind and rain.

I continued to play the piano for the church services while I remained there. The church ladies contacted each other, and held a work night. They were determined to put together a scrapbook with a page or two for each family, including some who had already PCS'd (permanent change of station) out and lived in other countries. When I taught ladies' Bible study for the last time, they presented it to me as a gift. I treasure it. I couldn't have asked for a better departing gift with so many memories woven into each page.

The day the Japanese moving van pulled up in front of my house, I realized God's eraser was removing the last part of my seven years stay in Japan. Several church men made a chain and the boxes were soon loaded. I summoned strength and faith as the van pulled away to carry my things to docks that I would never see. "Please Lord, take care of my things," I whispered in my heart.

Later that day, some friends took me to the airport. We arrived early and enjoyed lunch, a pedicure and manicure, and lots of laughs. At last we circled, prayed, cried, and said our final good-byes. With my ministry concluded, I took the moving steps downstairs and stood in the customs line to turn in my papers for the final time. I boarded the plane and returned to United States soil to begin the next chapter of my life.

～

From the neighbor performing CPR on Warren to his body arriving in the States, the Lord maneuvered just the right people to step in at the exact moment needed to help me along my journey.

Although Warren's spirit is in heaven, his body is buried in a military section of the Desert Lawn Cemetery in Kennewick, Washington, where his name is engraved on a granite wall with other veterans. A canon stands as a silent sentinel, signifying his "Mission Accomplished."

Christ has shown Himself faithful to me, as the years have rolled by since my husband's passing. He will do the same for you, my dear, widowed friend.

Memories

"The memory of the just is blessed..." (Prov. 10:7a).

Reflect on These Questions

CHAPTER 1 QUESTIONS

Funeral Information

1. When and where did your husband die?

2. Was your husband's death expected?
   If so, how long did you deal with grieving issues?

3. Where is your husband buried, and what is on/or planned for his tombstone?

4. What specific advice did a friend, funeral director, or a pastor give you, which helped and blessed you?

5. What life changing decisions were reached as a result of your husband's funeral service? *(Someone got saved, an estranged family member or friend attended and decided to rejoin the family, etc.)*

Hug This

"Precious in the sight of the LORD is the death
of his saints" (Ps. 116:15).

Additional comprehensive questions are provided in
chapter one of:

A Companion Journal,
Good Grief—I Need Relief! A Widow's Guide to
Recovering and Rejoicing.

Chapter Two

∽ Am I Going Crazy? ∼
God Talk from Job

Have you had even a passing thought, "I think I'm going crazy?"

I have! The endless paperwork, the chores, and learning new things with a foggy brain are difficult at best. But throw in having to do what my husband used to do on top of what we usually did together, and it seems to make my shoulders and spirits droop.

Grief throws havoc, chaos, and misery into our life so that we have trouble focusing, remembering things, and making wise choices. Confusion makes it difficult to function with purpose and waylays our well-intended plans. After awhile, we start thinking and even asking, "What is wrong with me? Am I going crazy? Why can't I handle life?"

No, you aren't going crazy!

When stress hits our life, it triggers hormonal reactions in our body, which prepare it to cope with extreme circumstances such as death or frightening situations. These elements put our muscles and brain on high alert, which is good. However, extended periods of stress affect the brain in adverse ways and impair memory and reasoning.

What can we do to make sure that we aren't stuck in the vice of stress? Treat ourselves with kindness and do something that is enjoyable. Lighten up on things that can wait to be done until another time. We can simplify our life through prayer, rest, and exercise, which seem to help overcome the bad effects of long-term stress.

A godly example of someone who didn't allow stress to control his life is Job. He rebutted the wrongful accusations of his well-meaning but wretched friends; things that perhaps we might have thought or even wished we could say to some friends who made mindless comments to us. ("After all, it's been a year..."). At least most comforters don't keep hanging around and continue to harass us as they did Job.

Would I have reacted like Job to news that my animals were destroyed or stolen, my servants and my ten children were dead? Would I have torn my outer garment, shaven my head, and fallen down and worshipped the Lord? He said, "Naked came I out of mother's womb, and naked shall I return thither: the LORD gave, and the LORD hath taken away; blessed be the name of the LORD" (Job 1:20-21).

No, my spirituality doesn't match Job's at all. God knew whom He could trust with that type of situation to bring Himself glory.

Yet Job talked to God in a way that seems rather incongruous to me—but to him it seemed right. Since God said that Job, "sinned not, nor charged God foolishly" (Job 1:22), then God didn't take offense. I guess it's all right for me to think, even say, some of the same things. But I want my walk close enough to Him that it seems natural to talk that way, and doesn't sound presumptuous or cocky.

How's your thought life? Are you foggy, depressed, mixed up, moody, suicidal, or perhaps negative? Job had some dark thoughts. If you haven't studied his life, these questions will give you an insight into how he spoke and lived. (The bold print has been added for emphasis.)

ANSWERS FROM JOB

Referenced by chapter

1. **Job 3:** Have you ever wondered **why you were born**? Job questioned his birth and cursed that day. He continued for several verses, saying how unhappy he was about living and wishing that he had never been born. He further says in Job 10:18b-19, "Oh that I had given up the ghost, and no eye had seen me! I should have been as though I had not been; I should have been carried from the womb to the grave."

2. **Job 6:** Has your thought life included asking the Lord to **just take you to heaven** to be with your husband? Do you feel that it is unfair that your husband was taken and you were left here to fend for yourself in this crazy world? I've thought, *why didn't he take us at the same time? Then we could all be rejoicing in heaven together, right?* I guess we will have to wait for that answer until we get there. Job wanted God **to destroy him** (6:9).

3. Do you feel that your friends should show some **sympathy and pity** for you? Do you feel afflicted and overwhelmed? Job joins you in those feelings, plus he felt his friends had dug a pit for him (6:14, 27).

4. **Job 7:** Have you thought your days were filled with **no hope**? Have you had anguish of your spirit and complained to God with bitterness in your soul? Job raises his hand to say "Yes" (7:6, 11).

5. Have you ever been so **sleepy** that you couldn't wait to get to bed, but when you did you couldn't go to sleep and tossed and turned all night? Or have you slept and had **scary dreams** so that you dreaded night? Job did both. However, he had such terrifying dreams and visions that, "His soul chose strangling, and death rather than life" (7:13-15).

6. **Job 9:** Some widows are **afraid to grieve.** They won't face the fact that their husband is gone and they won't allow their minds to go in a hurtful

direction, because they fear their grief might lead to overpowering emotions that they can't control. Job tells us in 9:28a, "I am afraid of all my sorrows, I know that thou wilt not hold me innocent."

7. **Job 10:** Are you **bitter** about your situation as a widow? Do you complain so much that other people see you coming and want to go the opposite direction? Job said his soul was weary of his life and he spoke in the bitterness of his soul (10:1).

8. Do you feel you are **condemned**? Job told God, "Do not condemn me" (10:2).

9. Have you complained to God that He is **destroying** your happy routine? Job spoke to God and said, "You made me yet you destroy me" (10:8).

10. Are you **confused** about the issues of life and just what the Lord has in mind for you? Job admitted, "I am full of confusion" (10:15).

11. **Job 12:** Do you ever want to **tell off your well-meaning friends**? Job took the liberty to do just that. I have to laugh when I read it; he **rebuts** his friend, Zophar, "No doubt but ye are the people, and wisdom shall die with you" (12:2).

12. How does the **darkness** affect you? Job tells us, "He (God) discovereth deep things out of darkness, and bringeth out to light the shadow of death" (12:22).

13. **Job 13:** Do you **agree** with Job's famous statement, "Though he slay me, yet will I trust in him: but I will

maintain mine own ways before him" (13:15)? Job holds onto his integrity before God.

14. Have you tried to **bargain with God**? What things have you asked God to do or not do? Job said he wouldn't hide from God if He would, "Withdraw thine hand far from me: and let not thy dread make me afraid" (13:20-21).

15. **Job 14:** Do you consider your **days filled with trouble**? Our life is not long (as compared to the people who lived in Old Testament days), and Job says they are "full of trouble" (14:1).

16. During your **grief,** do you agree that, "We come as a flower and are cut down and we flee like a shadow, and don't continue" (14:2)?

17. Have you ever felt **God is angry with you** and He won't listen? Job wanted, "God to hide him in the grave until his wrath passed and then at a set time to remember him" (14:13).

18. **Job 16:** Were some of the people who tried to comfort you with kind words really "**miserable comforters**" as Job called his friends? (16:2).

19. If you could trade places with some of the people who didn't comfort you in a good way, how would you treat them? Job told his friends that if they traded places, he could heap words against them and shake his head at them, but he wouldn't. Instead he would **strengthen them with his words to lessen their grief** (16:4-5). That should be everyone's goal,

but some people aren't sure just what to say to someone recently widowed or someone who dissolves into tears whenever someone mentions their loved one's name.

20. Do you feel young and spry or do you feel you have **aged considerably through your loss**? Do you have less hair and more wrinkles? Have you lost weight? Does it show in your face? Job confirms that he had not felt like eating. "And thou hast filled me with wrinkles, which is a witness against me: and my leanness rising up in me beareth witness to my face" (16:8).

21. Do you feel **God has torn you apart**? Job felt God tore him in His wrath and hated him (16:9).

22. **Were you complacent** before your husband died and now your life is upside down? Job said, "I was at ease, but he hath broken me asunder: he hath also taken me by my neck, **and shaken me to pieces**, and **set me up for his mark**" (16:12).

23. Have you felt like you were **run over** by a steamroller? Job felt like he had been run upon by a giant (16:14).

24. Job said his, "Eyelids had the **shadow of death** on them" (16:16). How would you describe your feelings?

25. Do your **friends snub or reject you?** Job's friends scorned him and his eyes poured out tears unto God (16:20). Perhaps they wondered what Job had done

to deserve the wrath of God so that all of his children died at once.

26. **Job 17: How are your eyes?** Job's eyes were affected by his grief (17:7).

27. Some widow's **feel that their** happy days and maybe their **purpose in life is over.** Job felt his days were past, his purposes broken off, even the thoughts of his heart (17:11).

28. Have you had **trouble sleeping?** Job did (17:12).

29. Job asked, "Where is now my hope?" (17:15). Do you feel all **hope is gone?**

30. **Job 19:** Have people told you it was time to **get over your grief and move on?** Job reproved his friends for tormenting him, asked how long they would vex or torment his soul, and said they had reproached or shamed him ten times (19:2-3).

31. Job found many negative things to say about the way he had been treated:

    • Job said God had overthrown him and compassed him with His net (19:6).

    • His cries weren't heard (19:7).

    • God fenced up his way so he couldn't pass, and set darkness in his paths (19:8).

    • God stripped him of his glory and took the crown from his head (19:9).

- He destroyed him on every side and removed his hope like a tree (19:10).

- God kindled his wrath against him and counted him as an enemy. His troops were round about him and against him (19:11-12).

- His kin failed him and friends forgot him (19:14).

- Those in his household thought of him as a stranger and an alien (19:15).

- He called his servant but he didn't answer (19:16).

- His breath was strange to his wife (19:17).

- Young children despised him and spoke against him (19:18).

- His close friends abhorred him and those he loved turned against him (19:19).

- His bones clung to his skin and flesh and he escaped with the "skin of his teeth" (19: 20).

- He asked the mourners to pity him for God's hand had touched him (19:21).

32. **Job 21:** we learn **Job felt God dealt unfairly with him** compared to how God treated other people.

- Job felt his mourning friends mocked him (21:3).

- He admitted his complaint was not with men; if it had been, his spirit would have troubled him (21:4).

- His memory makes him afraid and his flesh trembles (21:6).

- He questions why the wicked live and grow old and have mighty power; their children live and they see them. They don't fear and God's rod isn't on them (21:7-9).

- The wicked men's cattle prosper; he lost his livestock (21:10).

- Others have several children who dance and rejoice with musical instruments (21:11-12).

- Others are wealthy; he lost his wealth (21:13).

- They don't desire God and tell Him to leave them alone (21:14).

- They question who God is and why they should serve Him, or pray to Him (21:15).

- Job says God gives sorrows in His anger (21:17).

- Job said some people die in full strength, at ease and quiet; others die in bitterness of soul and never eat with pleasure. Yet they have the same end (21:23, 25-26).

33. **Job 23:**

- Job wished he knew where to find God because he would not plead against Him; he would argue with Him and God would strengthen him (23:3-6).

- He couldn't find God going forward, backward, on his left or right (23:8-9).

- "But he knoweth the way that I take: when he hath tried me, I shall come forth as gold" (23:10).

- Job kept God's way and didn't decline nor go back from His commandments (23:11-12).

- He realized he couldn't turn God's mind and He did as His soul desired (23:13).

- He acknowledged God performs the thing He appointed for him (23:14).

- God's presence troubled Job and when he considered it, he was afraid of Him and troubled (23:15-16).

34. **Job 27:**

- God took away His judgment and the Almighty vexed his soul. As long as Job lived, he said, "My lips shall not speak wickedness, nor my tongue utter deceit" (27:2-4).

- "My righteousness I hold fast, and will not let it go: my heart shall not reproach me so long as I live" (27:18).

35. **Job 28:** Job claimed, "The price of wisdom is above rubies" (28:18).

36. **Job 29:** Job thinks back on his life before the death of his children and the things that he enjoyed then. (Can you empathize with him?)

- Job laments by wishing for the past, the days God preserved him (29:2).

- God caused His light to shine upon Job as he walked through darkness (29:3).

- He longed for his youth when God was with him and his children about him (29:4-5).

- He lived in wealth with his steps washed in butter; he was known, acknowledged, and respected. His wisdom influenced princes and nobles (29:6-10).

- He reasoned his esteemed position was because he delivered the poor, fatherless, and those with no one to help them (29:11-12).

- The blessing of the perishing came on him and "he caused the widow's heart to sing for joy" (29:13).

- He lived "as a king in the army, as one that comforteth the mourners" (29:25).

37. **Job 30:**

- Job felt that young people, whose fathers he disdained, had him in derision. They were children of fools. Now Job is their byword, and they abhor him, flee far away, and spit in his face (30:1, 8-10).

- He felt God cast him into the mire, and he became like dust and ashes (30:19).

- He cried to God and didn't receive an answer (30:20).

- He said God was cruel to him (30:21).

- He wept for those in trouble and his soul grieved for the poor (30:25).

- When he looked for good; evil came (30:26).

- He mourned without the sun and cried in the congregation (30:28).

- His music turned to mourning (30:31).

Job's emotions, intertwined, knotted and twisted like several spools of thread, smoothed out when he listened to God and prayed for his miserable comforters. God blessed him again. He will do the same for us when we turn our tangled emotions over to Him to sort out.

---

*M*emories

"For he shall deliver the needy when he crieth; the poor also, and him that hath no helper" (Ps. 72:12).

Reflect on These Questions

CHAPTER 2 QUESTIONS

Am I Going Crazy?

1. Have you ever felt like you were going crazy?
    What situation/s made you feel that way?

2. Job felt God dealt unfairly with him compared to how
    God treated other people. Do you empathize with
    him? If yes, in what way?

3. Instead of internalizing your situation, have you tried
    to help other widows in mourning? How did you reach
    out?

4. What advice would you like to give some of your
    family members so they can better understand what
    you are going through, or have been through?

$\mathcal{C}$ount on $\mathcal{I}$t

"Behold, we count them happy which endure. Ye have heard of the patience of Job, and have seen the end of the Lord; that the Lord is very pitiful, and of tender mercy"
(James 5:11)

Additional comprehensive questions are provided in chapter two of:

A Companion Journal,
Good Grief—I Need Relief! A Widow's Guide to
Recovering and Rejoicing.

Chapter Three

∽ COMFORT ∽
HOW OTHER WIDOWS SURVIVED

*H*ave you ever wondered how other widows coped with their grief? Why do they appear to have things all together? How have they managed better or traveled further in their grief journey than you?

Here are some ways that widows answered the question, "What helped you move on after your husband died?"

- "When I was at a loss on how to cope with grief, I remember being in my backyard and talking out loud to God, 'Ok, Lord...what now...you can see I need help...' He said, 'You will be fine with my help.'"
- "My journey took me to think about friends who had also lost a husband recently. I invited them to lunch on my patio, and then kept up with them. There was a lot of talk about the hurt. What I noticed was I was progressing faster than my friends. Reaching out to help others and not focusing on my loss helped me."

- "I kept going to church."
- "I wanted to be with people."
- "I stayed with my dad when I could. I still get sad sometimes when I remember the past now that my dad has passed away too."
- "I kept busy working, cleaning, and going to church whenever the doors were open."
- "Reading when I can. Keeping KOLU (kolu.com, our Christian radio station) on day and night and I still do."
- "Talking on the phone with my sisters and other relatives."
- "When my husband died, I was in such shock that I felt like I was in a bad dream and couldn't wake up. I could have crawled in a corner and become a hermit, but the kids and grandkids were such a help and comfort. It was a blessing to be so loved. I don't know what I would have done without the Lord and the kids' encouragement. Keeping busy helped—but it seemed like it took so much to motivate me."
- "Faithful friends. Good pastor. More dependence on the Lord. Having family there for the first week or so to distract me."
- "There was a big blank after my husband died, so I kept busy. I went from the typewriter to knitting, and listened to music. I stayed in church. Later my pastor asked if I would take in a boarder, so she moved into a spare bedroom and we enjoyed each other's company.

When I moved out of town to be with family, she helped me pick out some things I needed."

- "For a year, I left the house after my son went to school and walked to a friend's house and helped her in her daycare. I don't know what I would have done without her. I also invited special singing groups or missionaries that visited our church to stay in my home."

- "I became closer to the Lord and prayed more. He and the cat were the only ones who wanted to listen!"

- "Getting up and knowing I had to do something helped me."

- "I began developing friendships with single women."

- "While going through my parents' things I saw how they planned for us kids, and knew that I needed to start thinking about the future and being realistic about it. I needed to allow other people, as my neighbors, to help me with things such as my computer or TV, or even opening a jar of pickles." (These thoughts are from a widow who had to go through her parents things after her mother died. She then realized how fragile her life was and that she needed to be willing to accept help and to prepare herself for the future, as she had no children).

- "I helped a local service club organize Christmas gifts that were given to the Veterans Affairs facilities. My contribution was knitting mittens."

- "I didn't get away from home right away. Because my husband was a teacher, many people, including students, came by my house to see me. After six months, I slowly started going back to rejoin my four different groups of friends."

- "Some things from the past bothered me, and I wanted to clear them up. So I prayed and the Lord showed me a slightly opened door. As I searched through some of my things, one day I found a Valentine that read, 'I Love You, (From) Me.' Later an inside door in my house slammed shut all by itself, and I knew that the issue was closed forever, just like that door."

- "I got into the Word, and attended Bible studies. I needed a lot of changing, and the Holy Spirit did it."

- "Through the whole time, my family and I stayed close. My daughter and I went to Paris—a wish fulfilled."

- "In Mexico, no one takes care of the gravesite; each family is responsible for their own upkeep. I keep my husband's site looking nice out of love for him, and respect for my family as well as it being a good testimony to the community."

- "I gave his clothes to pastors and to my children."

Mrs. Karen Kalapp, whose deceased husband, Doug, directed the Teams Missions Ministry at First Baptist Church in Hammond, Indiana, shares:

- The greatest help of all was walking with the Lord each day.

- When I continued to write on the Carepages and share with others how God was helping me, it in turn helped others. Knowing that I was helping others was a great healing factor.
- Soul winning always helps to heal.
- I believe I started healing more when I started teaching a Sunday school class again.
- Staying close to family and to my church family was very important.
- Friends were very important. I have a friend who lost her husband exactly one month before I lost my husband. She came by the house on the day I came home from the hospital (where her husband died) and asked if we could be friends. Her friendship has been invaluable to me as we have gone soul winning, visited widows, and even gone on short vacations together. We have had many talks and have encouraged each other greatly.
- I think it helped me to start getting real closure when I moved out of the house my husband and I lived in and I finally lived alone. It forced me to depend even more on the Lord and helped me to start getting closure. I am still in this process, so that's why I say I'm not sure I have completely moved on yet.
- While still living at my first house with my daughter and her family, my little granddaughter Emma was born, with Down syndrome. Children with Down syndrome are so very special—they almost seem like

little angels from heaven. Each night I would come home and hold Emma, and it was very healing to my heart.

⸺

Mrs. Vicky Pass, a widowed pastor's wife in Salem, Oregon, said, "Although I knew the verse, absent from the body, and...present with the Lord' (2 Cor. 5:8), the year my pastor husband died, it was a bleak winter and I didn't like the idea that he had been put into the ground and it was dark and cold there. God gave me victory that, 'He wasn't in the grave.' Then I started thinking more about what he might be doing in heaven, and who he might be talking with."

Comfort

"Wherefore comfort yourselves together, and edify one another, even as also ye do" (1 Thess. 5:11).

Reflect on These Questions

CHAPTER 3 QUESTIONS

Comfort—How You Survived

1. Your story is probably very different from the ones you just read, and might be a bit unusual too. In what areas did/do you struggle?

2. Tell about your victories.

3. To whom did you reach out for comfort?

4. Name the main people who reached out to you.

5. Which of the many ideas that other widows used to move forward did you incorporate into your life?

*S*upport

"I know, O LORD, that thy judgments are right, and that
thou in faithfulness hast afflicted me. Let, I pray thee, thy
merciful kindness be for my comfort, according to thy
word unto thy servant. Let thy tender mercies come unto
me, that I may live: for thy law is my delight"
(Ps. 119:75-77).

Additional comprehensive questions are provided in
chapter three of:

A Companion Journal,
Good Grief—I Need Relief! A Widow's Guide to
Recovering and Rejoicing.

Chapter Four

∽ TRAVELING ∽
GREAT AS A COUPLE,
DAUNTING AS A SINGLE

*W*arren and I left the United States when most people our age were retiring. Instead, the Lord elected to place us in Tokyo, Japan. We left all of our family and friends behind, and eagerly anticipated the many new friends with whom we would connect in the future.

My journey as a widow began on March 17, 2008. As missionaries to the U.S. military, Warren and I served seven years before the Lord took him home. We were three years shy from celebrating our fiftieth wedding anniversary.

One day in Japan we needed to travel downtown and we got lost. Japan does not have on and off ramps like we do here in the States and we drove many extra miles before we finally found our way safely back home.

Imagine bumper-to-bumper traffic and no place to park, and that will give you a mental image of Japan.

Another time when we got lost, Warren had dropped me off at a convenience store so I could ask directions while he continued to drive around the block. I said to the clerk, "Can you please tell me how to get to the Yokota Air Force Base?" I figured the Base name was well known and it was easier than giving him my address, and when we got close to the Base, we would know where we were, and could go straight home. The clerk immediately got out a map, went to his copier, made a copy, and then kindly highlighted the road to the Base. God is so good to His children.

Now I reminisce and enjoy pictures from the many places we traveled together: Egypt, Israel, Japan, Jordan, Mexico, and the Philippine Islands. Each one impacted our lives in a different way. We lived in Alabama, Georgia, Idaho, Tennessee, Washington, and two foreign countries: Canada and Japan. Throughout the years, we traveled most of the continental states.

Two particular international trips stand out to me. The first was when a friend gifted me so that I could accompany my husband to Israel on a trip-of-a-lifetime with our church family.

The second journey taught us coping skills. We ate strange food in an unknown culture, and heard a language we couldn't understand while living for nine weeks in Okinawa, Japan, filling in for a missionary couple who needed a short furlough. (The electricity went out and we couldn't speak the language; that proved an interesting challenge. Fortunately, the missionaries left us their landlord's phone number and we went to a neighbor's house and tried to explain we needed help! The Lord took care of it for us and the lights were finally restored.) That experience laid the foundation for the years that the Lord used us as missionaries in mainland Japan.

I have sweet memories of my life's partner as my traveling companion. To be able to scan a crowd and see him waiting for me always quickened my pulse and gave me a feeling of security. We walked many airports together, shared thoughts during airport layovers, held hands as our flights took off, and his shoulder cradled my head perfectly as I slept during our trips.

Now when I travel, I want to be sure that I don't touch the person next to me, or fall asleep and wake up on a stranger's shoulder, and I always take my purse with me to the bathroom to be sure that nothing is taken while I am away.

I have traveled alone several times since my husband died, and the Lord has taken great care of me, and given me opportunities to share the gospel with lonely people.

My daughter gifted me with a cruise and we made precious memories. She and I had a great time together although we took turns getting sick.

Although my beloved doesn't live with me anymore, I can recall the special places we visited together, and praise the Lord for those treasures.

Hug This

"Teach me thy way, O Lᴏʀᴅ; I will walk in thy truth: unite my heart to fear thy name" (Ps. 86:11).

Reflect on These Questions

CHAPTER 4 QUESTIONS

Traveling

1. What states and countries have you visited?

2. How did you financially prepare for your trips (e.g. by saving monthly, borrowing, using air miles, or gifted by a friend)?

3. Where did you go on your most pleasant trip?

4. What made it memorable?

5. What new locations are on your bucket list?

*S*hare

Share your memories with the Lord and rejoice together for the times that you enjoyed on your trips, whether they were exotic, to a grocery store, or a ball game. Grasp and hold them, as they are the ticket to your memory bank.

*T*ell *H*im

"I will praise thee, O Lord my God, with all my heart: and I will glorify thy name for evermore" (Ps. 86:12).

Additional comprehensive questions are provided in chapter four of:

A Companion Journal,
Good Grief—I Need Relief! A Widow's Guide to
Recovering and Rejoicing.

Chapter Five

∾ HEALTH ∾
HOW'S YOURS?

*A*fter Warren died, I started working as the missionary assistant in the missions department at the Riverview Baptist church where I attended. Sometimes I got busy and didn't always eat like I should have. It just didn't seem that important. I could identify with the psalmist, who said, "My heart is smitten, and withered like grass; so that I forget to eat my bread" (Ps. 102:4).

The results? I lost weight and people around me noticed it before I did. Some made comments, "If you turn sideways, the wind could blow you away." Or, "Are you still losing weight? I hope not." Perhaps remarks meant in a kind way, but nevertheless emotionally challenging.

As I progressed in my grief journey, I realized my clothes at times looked liked they had been super-sized and I needed to make some changes. I loved the challenge of shopping for bargains to see what kind of outfits I could put together for as little money as possible.

I found that when the sun didn't smile and the day appeared drab, I could perk myself up a bit by dressing in brighter colors, wearing jewelry, etc. As I looked in the mirror before I left for work each day, I wanted, and needed, to see a reflection that encouraged, pleased, and gave me confidence. I didn't want to appear in the throes of mourning, even though I knew I was. Perhaps that helped give the appearance that I progressed faster in my journey of recovery than people figured I might.

PANIC ATTACK

One day in December, I had what I later analyzed as a grief or panic attack. I sat in a parking lot and had difficulty breathing and a terrible pain smashed my chest; I couldn't take a deep breath. I started crying, praying, and begging, "Please, Lord, just beam me up!" He chose not to, and I gasped for air for quite awhile until the pain gradually subsided.

It reoccurred again at the chiropractor's office later that day, and he tried everything he could think of to help me, and then finally sent me to the emergency room. The diagnosis? Pleurisy. I was given a couple of prescriptions for pain pills and told to see my primary doctor.

Later I assessed myself and came to the conclusion the whole thing was stress related. Now I could have scolded myself and said, "What's wrong with you? You just need to buck up and learn to lean on the Lord more.

This is ridiculous! You are a Christian, where's your faith? You can do this!" But the truth of the matter is that when we do things in our own strength and don't allow ourselves time to grieve, we can get in a real mess.

At times the Lord wants us to be alone and allow Him to fill the emptiness and loneliness with His presence. If we are constantly busy with other people, we can't hear His voice, and it is difficult to grieve. We have no time to go back over our life and review the different seasons as: newlyweds, child rearing, family weddings, empty nesters, and grandchildren, and perhaps the plans that we might have made for retirement years.

TWICE BLESSED

In Japan I had internal colon polyps removed and the doctor said some looked suspicious. I waited two weeks to find out they were not cancerous. At that time, Warren said, "Praise the Lord," when we were told the good news.

Eleven months after my husband passed away, I had polyps removed from my throat.

"Praise the Lord," I said, when the nurse told me two days later that they were benign! This time I said it alone, but both times, the Lord gave me great peace before I found out the results. It was a blessing the second time over.

Hints

- If you suffer from pain, I found a TENS Device (Transcutaneous Electrical Nerve Stimulation) to be helpful. My physical therapist recommended it for my back pain, my doctor approved it, and my insurance paid for it. I have since learned that such a device is available cordless and is accessible through a catalog without a doctor's approval (of course you pay). Search online for further information.

- For a breakfast on-the-run type morning, I make a smoothie with some of my favorite fruits (fresh when they are available) such as blueberries, strawberries, bananas, plus flavored or plain yogurt, and a little peanut butter added for some protein. Yum!

- Be sure to get an annual health check up to stay on top of any health issues that arise which you might not even be aware of. Also see your dentist and ophthalmologist.

- Kick start your day with exercises. It will help the blood flow to your brain, and stimulate your thinking processes.

- Keep learning new things each day to help ward off dementia.

- I drink water right before bedtime and keep some by my bed at night so I can get a drink when I wake up with a dry mouth. I have learned that water also helps lessen my leg cramps, as does taking magnesium.

- Using an inclined pillow at night reduced my acid reflux rather than taking medication for it.

Consider

"What time I am afraid, I will trust in thee" (Ps. 56:3).

Reflect on These Questions

CHAPTER 5 QUESTIONS

Health

1. What particular health issue/issues did you have before your husband died?

2. Were these issues stress related, age related, or inherited?

3. Did you have an issue with eating when you began eating alone?

4. What is the greatest health problem you battle right now? Are you making progress and improving?

5. Have you done research to learn if there is a new method, treatment, or drug that might benefit you?

Ponder

"What? Know ye not that your body is the temple of the Holy Ghost which is in you, which ye have of God, and ye are not your own? For ye are bought with a price: therefore glorify God in your body, and in your spirit, which are God's" (1 Cor. 6:19-20).

Additional comprehensive questions are provided in chapter five of:

A Companion Journal,
Good Grief—I Need Relief! A Widow's Guide to
Recovering and Rejoicing.

Chapter Six

∽ SLEEP, REST, & NAPS ∽
BRING THEM ON

$\mathcal{D}$octors tell us that we should get seven or more hours of sleep a night so that our brain can work efficiently. We think properly and concentrate better when we get the amount of rest that our body functions require.

I found it difficult to fall asleep at night due to the added stress of the many decisions that I faced as a widow. For a while, I took a natural sleep aid. However, even small dosages seemed to leave residual effects the next day. So I decided that I would rather be able to think clearly with less sleep and take a nap during the day, than to try to fight the foggy brain that seemed to linger when I took something to help me relax and fall asleep.

Unless really necessary, prescription drugs are not recommended. Grief is difficult, but something that widows have to go through. Healing comes when issues are faced and dealt with, not by medicating the mind so that it temporarily pushes away or clouds our pain and prolongs grief.

Many days I find a short nap (I set a timer for about seventeen to twenty minutes) picks me up and allows me to be able to finish projects. If I doze for too long, I find it difficult to wake up and get busy again and then I don't want to get in bed at a practical hour, and it starts a vicious cycle.

Do you need a new mattress, mattress topper, or pillow to aid you in sleeping better? I replaced my pillows and mattress, and found it helped my back pain because my spine was better supported.

Try to establish a regular and reasonable bedtime schedule; it signals your body to slow down and relax.

Tips for Relaxing

- Prepare your bedroom to be used only for sleep. I don't do bookwork, exercise (as on a treadmill), or read in my bedroom before I go to bed. I recommend removing the TV, so when you walk into your room, the bed beckons you to lie down and rest. Make it as pretty and inviting as you can; it is your sleep haven.
- Listen to soothing music.
- Relax with some Chamomile tea.
- If you like to use an alarm clock, make sure it has red letters because it is more calming than green ones.
- Take a relaxing bath.

- Watch a funny movie to get your mind off of the cares of the day.

- Use lavender lotion (or a fragrance of your choice) each night right before bed as it signals your body that it's time to relax.

- Make sure your room is darkened. For daytime naps, a dark sleep mask is ideal.

THINGS THAT DETRACT FROM SLEEP:

- Except for mild stretches, most exercising should be done earlier in the day as it energizes your body instead of calming it.

- Working on social media, or anything that energizes the mind, makes it difficult to go right to sleep since the brain wants to rehash what you have just done.

$\mathcal{H}$int

I found by nighttime that my mind and body were frazzled, so I made a list of things to do for the next day. It usually included paperwork and problem solving items, which seemed easier in the daylight hours.
Also, if I needed input from a friend, I could feel free to reach them for advice.

Once you're in bed, thank the Lord for at least five specific blessings from your day, or life in general; then pray and tell Him good night.

Here are some general praise suggestions in case you draw a blank: time spent with your husband, how many anniversaries you shared, health, home, happiness, friends, family reunions, seasons, heaven, transportation, holidays, vacations, church family, prayer groups, Christian radio, God's Word, down-time, naps, sage advice, writers, teachers, pastors, missionaries, freedom, clothing, memories, new experiences, memory of past experiences.

⌒

Fifteen months after becoming a widow, my journal records that during the night, "I felt strong demon oppression and started to sing, 'Jesus Loves Me.' It immediately stopped. I turned on our church's Christian radio station, KOLU, and left it on for the rest of the night. It was comforting."

Another journal entry states, "I have decided I cannot continue to live in the past, as wonderful as it was with Warren. I can never go back; I will never be his wife again and minister to the military in Japan. It is so hard to close that chapter of my life. I acknowledge so with tears in my eyes."

*R*est on *T*hese

"It is vain for you to rise up early, to sit up late, to eat the bread of sorrows: for so he giveth his beloved sleep" (Ps. 127:2).

"I will both lay me down in peace, and sleep: for thou, LORD, only makest me dwell in safety" (Ps. 4:8).

Reflect on These Questions

CHAPTER 6 QUESTIONS

Sleep, Rest, and Naps

Can you usually accomplish most of your to-do list or the projects you have planned when you get enough sleep or a nap? If not, it's time to reevaluate; do you expect too much from yourself?

1. How many hours of rest do you think you need to feel your best?

2. Do you have your bedroom set up so that you relax when you walk in?   What can you do to make it more beautiful?

3. When you have friends or family in overnight do you sleep better?   If yes, why?

4. What have you included in your nightly bedtime routine to help you relax?

5. Do you pray before you go to sleep and thank the Lord for at least five blessings from your day?

$\mathcal{R}est\ \mathcal{A}ssured$

"When thou liest down, thou shalt not be afraid: yea, thou shalt lie down, and thy sleep shall be sweet" (Prov. 3:24).

Additional comprehensive questions are provided in chapter six of:

A Companion Journal,
Good Grief—I Need Relief! A Widow's Guide to Recovering and Rejoicing.

Part Two

Looking Around

*"And all things, whatsoever ye shall ask in prayer,
believing, ye shall receive"*
(Matt. 21:22).

Chapter Seven

↶ A PRAYER PARTNER ↷
DO YOU HAVE ONE?

*W*arren and I grew up in families who practiced faith praying, believing that doing so resulted in answers from a God who cares and loves us.

We based our marriage and home life on the same biblical principles and took that practice with us to Tennessee where we attended Bible college. While there, God grew our faith as He answered prayer after prayer for a young family learning to lean on Him.

We prayed about where to live, where to serve, our educational needs, and hundreds of other things. How we grew from faith to faith in those days. After graduation, we saw our faith stretched more in the pastorate but God met our every need. What an awesome God who hears before we call.

Our faith accompanied our hearts to Japan, but bitterness crippled me and I was only liberated when I asked forgiveness a long time afterward. Here's how it happened.

When we visited Japan so my husband could candidate for the pastorate of the Yokota Baptist Church, he was accepted with only two dissenting votes. The head deacon came into the room where my husband and I waited and told us the results of the vote and asked my husband, "Do you accept the church vote to become our pastor?"

I looked at my husband fully expecting him to say, "My wife and I will pray about it and get back with you later." However, his immediate reply was, "I accept!"

I can't fully put into words what I felt at that moment—but happiness wouldn't describe it! I felt total shock. Perhaps my mouth didn't fall open and my eyes bug out physically, but they did inside. We had always prayed together about everything! How could he jump into this situation and ignore my thoughts and feelings?

He grabbed my hand and we left the waiting room as happy people crowded around to congratulate him. He rejoiced with the people and appeared on cloud nine. But in shocked pettiness, I drew aside and nursed my hurt feelings. I felt totally left out. One person saw me standing alone and gave me a hug.

Later I kept pushing the replay button. Each time it sounded something like, *I can't believe he accepted the church without praying with me. He didn't even ask me how I felt about the situation or if I wanted to accept the call to Japan! I can't believe this is happening...*

I kept up a façade so no one realized that I was unhappy with the current events, but I packed rebellion into my suitcase along with my clothes, when we returned to the U.S. for several months of deputation. (Notice I said several months!) Although I enjoyed the new people we met as we traveled from church to church, I missed out on so many blessings because I had an unforgiving heart.

As our support climbed and the time drew closer to leave the U.S., I thought of several evasive tactics. We needed to do this or that; we needed one more Christmas with our family, our son needed us, etc. Finally I ran out of excuses to keep us from leaving, and we began seriously packing our house. We held a yard sale and sold several things. Our pastor called and said, "I think you should save some basic furniture in case it doesn't work out for you and you have to come back." Little did we know we were storing things to help me set up housekeeping after I became a widow.

As they stacked box after box on the truck, I felt overwhelmed; things moved too quickly and I couldn't assimilate them. When the box with our Christmas decorations got stacked at the back of the truck, I had a meltdown. "Please, this is going too fast, I just can't handle it," I said and began crying. The truck driver, a man from our church, quickly said, "It's all right. I'll just leave the truck and you can finish later." I was so grateful.

My husband didn't seem to realize my hesitancy about leaving the United States, and I am ashamed to admit that when we arrived in Japan, my hardened heart arrived with me.

I accepted the things that my husband wanted me to do at the church, and willingly taught in the Christian school when he began one. However, as I sat under his preaching on Sundays, I pushed the replay button over and over. *Why wasn't I included in the decision to come here?* (Pretty petty, huh?)

Bitterness ruled my waking hours but no one knew it—except God. I didn't share it because I doubted anyone cared, would understand, or they might find my problem trivial or silly. Besides, a pastor's wife is expected to be in perfect agreement with her husband's decisions and I didn't want to put him in a bad light. I could see no way around or over the issue that now loomed as a mountain. Satan fueled my rebellion over and over. I didn't receive a blessing when I read the Bible and I had no fellowship with Christ.

How could I minister to the church ladies when I clung to bitterness?

Quite a while passed before I finally accepted the fact that my husband didn't have to pray with me before he said yes to the Lord! Who did I think I was that my husband had to have my permission to accept what he knew to be the Lord's will?

When I finally humbled myself and asked the Lord to forgive my bad spirit, joy returned and I once again enjoyed His word, a prayer life, and spiritual growth.

When I gained the courage, I told Warren about my turmoil. Although he had remained clueless about my struggle, he immediately apologized. We again became one in spirit and continued in the ministry with one accord.

A PRAYER PARTNER

When you speak someone's heart language, it's easy to share your burdens and then pray together. Warren and I maintained separate personal prayer lists, but shared the needs of our church family through our weekly updated prayer bulletins.

Our hearts were tenderized by the numerous burdens that the young military families carried with them to a foreign country. The young women grew weary and lonesome when their husband's were deployed and they had to keep the home fires burning without their mate. Then when he returned, they stepped back to follow him as the leader in the home again.

After Warren passed, I definitely missed that part of our closeness, the prayer opportunity that no longer existed.

Although I found it hard, I realized I needed a friend or friends with whom I could share my prayer requests. Why was that difficult? Because I tend to be a quiet person and it's not easy to share my thoughts, hurts, and interests with other people. I found it uncomfortable to air such issues with a ladies Bible study group. Yes, one-on-one was what I needed.

The Lord gave me two such friends. Suffice it to say, we have prayed each other through family discouragements, ministry decisions, and multiple other issues. What a blessing to call or text a friend and receive an immediate reply. What a privilege that after I had talked to the Lord, I could also get input from them and knew they wouldn't betray my confidence. What sweet fellowship we've enjoyed through the years.

I wish the same thing for you, dear widowed friend. Please ask the Lord to give you someone who cares, someone who will listen without being critical, and someone who won't pass on your information, or gossip about you.

Treasure These

"Again I say unto you, that if two of you shall agree on earth as touching any thing that they shall ask, it shall be done for them of my Father which is in heaven. For where two or three are gathered together in my name, there am I in the midst of them" (Matt. 18:19-20).

"A man that hath friends must shew himself friendly: and there is a friend that sticketh closer than a brother" (Prov. 18:24).

Reflect on These Questions

CHAPTER 7 QUESTIONS

A Prayer Partner

1. Did you and your husband pray together? What special answers stand out in your mind?

2. Whom has the Lord brought into your path that you have been able to share your heart-felt prayer requests with?

3. Is she/he a new friend? If so, where and when did you meet?

4. If it is someone you have known for a long time, record how long you have known this special friend and why you feel comfortable sharing your heart with them.

5. What topics have you discussed, cried, and prayed about together?

If you don't have such a friend, why not pray and ask the Lord to give you a dear friend in whom you can confide. Quote the verse below and see what happens.

Lean on This

"Ask, and it shall be given you; seek, and ye shall find; knock, and it shall be opened unto you: For every one that asketh receiveth; and he that seeketh findeth; and to him that knocketh it shall be opened" (Matt. 7:7).

Additional comprehensive questions are provided in chapter seven of:

A Companion Journal,
Good Grief—I Need Relief! A Widow's Guide to
Recovering and Rejoicing.

Chapter Eight

∽ HOME OWNERSHIP & REPAIRS ∽
YIKES!

*W*here could I live? I had no house or property.

While still settled in Japan, Warren and I talked about buying a house in the States, but nothing gave us an "Aha" moment. Now I faced the fact alone that I had no husband, and no place to live.

I called from Japan and talked to my mother, in her late eighties and currently residing in a retirement home, "Mom, would you like to buy a house together?"

"Yes, I would." Yay, I had someone to live with. I was delighted!

When I arrived in the States, we began searching for just the right house we believed the Lord had for us. The chorus, "The Lord Knows the Way through the Wilderness," became real to me and I realized just like the words said, "All I had to do was follow." It didn't end up quite that easy, but it did go well.

My pastor recommended a real estate lady who used to work with his wife; we met and began looking at homes. Later we became good friends because her husband, who helped make some repairs on our house, passed away also.

My two daughters flew in and helped me house hunt. We agreed on one that allowed mom and me to have separate living areas on each end of the house, and an area in the middle for eating and relaxing.

I called myself Gypsy Joyce because I lived out of a suitcase as I moved from house to house of relatives and friends for several weeks. To be exact, I stayed in twelve different places, which included a couple of hotels! After a journey of four months, we received the key and settled into our cozy, comfortable repo.

Did I mention that our backyard borders a freeway? The Lord must have struck me deaf every time we looked at the house, because I don't remember the backyard being noisy, but noisy it is. How could this happen? I just wanted quietness and solitude; you know the kind of peace where you step outside and the silence begs you to interrupt it-not busy, loud traffic going 70 mph behind my fence!

Did I question the Lord about peace? Absolutely.

What did He say? He impressed me that, "*Peace is found in Me, not in a place.*" Maybe He knew I might worship the silence more than I would Him. He is, after all, all knowing.

∽

Owning a home holds much more responsibility than I ever could have imagined. I don't know what I expected, but I soon came to realize that I had a whole lot of learning ahead of me. Here are some things I learned that might be helpful to you as a widow.

HOME BLESSING

A home dedication was one of the first things that I did when my mother and I bought a home together.

While living in Japan, I noticed the Japanese people used priests to pray over their land before they built on it. This was to dismiss evil spirits from that particular place. They also prayed for safety during construction of a house. They figured if something bad happened, then they had angered the god of the land.

I remember when our missionary friends in Okinawa, the Truitts, moved into their new apartment. I was impressed because they prayed in each room and dedicated it to the Lord.

Since I didn't know the builder or the former owner of our house, I decided that our home needed to be dedicated to the Lord too. Before our home had things in place, I invited a few friends and our pastor to come over after church and pray that the Lord would fill our home with joy, and that He would be honored and praised in it. We also prayed that any evil spirits who might be present leave (I had no idea if anyone had ever held a séance or some such there), and asked for His protection about our property. It was a joy-filled evening.

The plaque inside the living room next to my front door, reads: "Choose you this day whom ye will serve...but as for me and my house, we will serve the LORD" (Josh. 24:15).

UNPACKING

When my things finally cleared customs and were placed in the garage along with the boxes that had been stored for the seven years we were in Japan, then it became my monumental task as a widow to tackle the job of unpacking. Some semblance of order had to be made before winter so I could get my car in the garage.

One morning I walked into the garage very early and began moving a few of the boxes. I saw Warren's handwriting for the first time since his death—on boxes we had stored. It startled me and then an overwhelming emotion took over and I quickly retreated into the house. Winter or no winter, I had to wait until another day to calm down and face it again.

I knew I eventually had to do it and I managed to slowly work through most of the boxes. Then I called some preacher boys from the church I attended and asked them to go through Warren's book boxes and take as many as they wanted. I was happy to see they could use several of them.

REPAIRS

When our furniture was in place and real living set in, we discovered that there were some things that weren't exactly right in our new home and were in need of repair.

I trust that you are more inclined to repair things than I am. I was never taught practical things (why didn't they include that in home economics years ago?) as how to rewire a lamp, fix a loose screw in drywall, put together a bookcase, or a multitude of other things that seemed to scream "Help!" when I became a homeowner. Why can't things just remain status quo? Why do they break down, break loose, or wear out? Seems like I always had a "Honey-do List" with no honey to do it!

Take for instance the time I was getting ready for church and running late. I pushed the garage door opener and it acted crazy! It only went up about four feet and stopped. Later it went all of the way up. I replaced the remote battery and it still didn't work right. After I paid someone to come out to look at it a couple of times, I decided that the wall button had malfunctioned one too many times, and I bought another remote and mounted it beside the original. It worked like a charm, and there were no more service calls.

CHEAPEST IS NOT ALWAYS BEST

I am a frugal person. (Not cheap, frugal. Cheap is always trying to get the other person to foot the bill.) So when I went to the store to purchase a couple of ceiling fans, I decided that I would save a little bit and just get the least expensive ones. When the serviceman tried to install it, he couldn't get the wires down through something or other to work with a remote. (The remote was needed because we have vaulted ceilings and I didn't want to stand on my bed or a couch to pull a chain, or have one long enough to be dangling in a guest's face when they stood up.) So I relented and agreed he could get larger, nicer fans already programmed for their remote. They did look sharper when they were installed than the dinky ones I had chosen; and they worked well.

Lesson learned: Don't always assume the cheapest thing on the market is the best way to go and that it will work as well as something a bit pricier.

YARD WORK

My widowed friend knew I needed to get outside, so she finagled to come over and teach and help me take charge of my yard—to the neglecting of her own.

I remember as we worked the first day she said, "Are we having fun yet?"

Knowing I was in a foul mood and not enjoying my newly acquired widowed title, she laughed when I emphatically replied, "No!"

She returned numerous times and we worked in the yard, shopped together for several things I needed in the house, and she continued to encourage me.

THINGS TO PONDER:

- When buying new plants, bushes or trees:

  1. What size will they be when they mature?

  2. How much do they grow each year?

  3. How much sunlight do they require?

  4. How far from your house should you plant them so their root system won't interfere with your foundation?

  5. Will you be capable of maintaining them if they require pruning with heavy hedge trimmers, or will you have to hire help? Can you sharpen pruning shears if you need to or send them out to be sharpened?

- When purchasing flowers, do you want annuals such as petunias and geraniums (which must be replaced yearly) or do you want plants that will re-seed themselves each year such as snapdragons, alyssum, or bulbs as lilies, irises, or peonies?

- Consider how much water each variety needs.

- There are some types of moss that can be used as ground cover and they can be walked on without killing them.

- In early spring, check all underground sprinkler heads to be sure they weren't damaged by cold weather.

WEEDING

It's amazing how much can be accomplished in a few minutes of concentrated work each day to try to keep your yard weed free. I take a small section and weed it and the next day I look it over briefly and pull or spray any stragglers, and then I move on to another area.

Working early in the morning is a good idea if the weather is supposed to be extremely hot. If you work outside the home and have limited time, set a timer for the length of time you can spare and work in your yard before you shower and start your day. It will invigorate you!

PRUNING, PLANTING, AND WATERING

If you need help with pruning, planting, watering, or disease control, call a nursery, purchase a book about how to handle plants in your area, or borrow a library book.

If you need to track someone in your home while you are outside working, set up a baby monitor and give them a bell to ring which signals they need your help. Take the second monitor outside with you. It works well for giving both my mom and I peace when she is inside resting and I am outside working. I keep the monitor by my side, or hooked over my finger if I am watering.

My dermatologist reminded me, "Don't forget to use sunscreen." I add a garden hat, gloves, and long-sleeved shirts to have protection from the sun each day.

Tips

- Since I am sensitive to some of the bushes in my yard, I wear long garden gloves that come half way up my arms when I am pruning.

- I use a large plastic plant saucer to toss small weeds into. When it gets full, I empty it into a yard bag which I have used to line a large pot. If I am cutting down shrubs, I use a large pot or large cardboard box to poke long branches into.

MOWING

I started my yard experience by hiring a teen to mow for me, and then I bought a push mower and decided I could mow it myself for the exercise. As time passed, I realized that wasn't the kind of exercise that I enjoyed. Ok, truthfully I hated it and it physically wore me out. I bought a self-propelled mower and hired someone to mow and trim for me. It was a good call. I water and fertilize; they mow.

ASSEMBLING

I assisted my friend and we assembled things for my home I never dreamed I could manage: book cases, a wooden file cabinet, and a computer desk. She seemed to know how to do anything and said, "I fake it if I don't." We spent a lot of those days laughing, a wonderful way to release pent up grief feelings.

Hint

Always read through the complete instructions before you begin. Lay the pieces out and check to be sure everything is there. If something is missing or the instructions don't make sense, call their 800 number or go online and get the info you need right away. We found it helpful to use the dining room area for large projects, but a garage or patio would work as well. Consider the bulkiness and weight of your project to determine how easy it would be to move it back inside if you assemble it outside.

WINTER ISSUES

I was unprepared for the first winter in our new home when the heavens opened and dumped snow on our yard (which was fine) but the Lord got overzealous when He covered the driveway with layer upon layer of the beautiful white stuff. I shoveled more snow that winter than I had in my entire life. I tried to be thankful that I had the strength to do it, even when I got up early each morning to see if I needed to shovel before I left to go to work or to church.

One Sunday the snow was so deep that a couple of friends came and picked us up and drove us to church. When we returned, they finished shoveling where I left off, while I enjoyed fixing them a lunch.

Yard Winterizing Tips

- It's a good idea at the end of the lawn-mowing season to check your manual to see what maintenance you need to do before you store it.

- Cut back a few shrubs or trees each day or each week so that you can get it finished by the end of the season without a feeling of panic. For easy clean up for large pruning jobs, cover the ground under the tree or bush with a drop cloth. For smaller jobs, use a yard bag. Simply spread the plastic before you begin, and drag or fold it up when you are finished and toss it in the trash.

- Mulch around or over plants that need TLC. If you are not sure just what do, check online for care of your particular plants, or call a nursery, or ask a friend or neighbor for ideas.

- Drain garden hoses (if that is necessary, as it is in my zone), and store them in a shed or garage.

- Don't forget to clean the filter screen for your underground sprinkler system several times a season.

- Some people use Styrofoam covers on their outside faucets, but they have never worked well for me. They don't fit properly and they sometimes blow away.

If your yard work overwhelms you and you don't have family or friends to help, consider your options for eliminating it:

- Hire church or neighborhood teens

- Hire a lawn service

- Move in with your children

- Move to an apartment, condo, retirement home or a nursing home.

UPGRADES

We did several upgrades on our home after we moved in, including: more attic insulation; a covered patio extension, which helped save on the heating and air conditioning; wider steps going into the garage; and an iron railing added to the back concrete steps that allowed my aging mother easier access to the backyard. We also added a front screen door, a gate, garage shelving, curbing, a walk-in shower, and a security system.

In a moment of insanity, I had over half of the grass removed from the backyard with raised flowerbeds to replace it. Where I ever got the idea it would be easier to care for flowers than grass, I'll never know, because I have spent hours and hours pulling weeds from the flower beds! Gradually people started saying it looked like an English Garden. Little did they know the work involved through the years!

Now we are pleased with our little renovated home, and thank the Lord often for it.

He truly knows what we need—and when.

⌒

At the end of each year, purchase a desk or wall calendar and add the following things on it to help you organize your house, yard, and life. It will give you an idea of how to keep track of annual and monthly renewals. Your list can be tailor made for your situation.

- Birthdays: purchase ahead for the month
- Special occasions: weddings, graduations, anniversaries
- Holidays: decorations taken out/put away, cards mailed
- Utility bills: due monthly or every two months
- Magazine renewals
- Car tabs
- Insurance premium renewals: set up new insurance log-ins if changed

You can also add house maintenance chores:

- Change clocks and fire alarm batteries every six months, around daylight savings time
- Furnace filters
- Sprinklers blown out in the fall and turned on in the spring
- Christmas lights up outside
- Christmas tree up/taken down
- Air conditioner/furnace servicing for the year
- Air ducts cleaned: reduces allergens, dust, mold
- Clothes dryer duct cleaned
- Carpets cleaned
- Windows cleaned

- Fireplace chimney cleaned out
- Clean under stove
- Clean behind refrigerator
- Water filter changed
- Gutters and downspout cleaned out: twice a year if there are lots of trees around, or in the fall after leaves finish falling
- Fencing repaired
- Launder large comforters before and after cold season
- Clean light fixtures
- Bushes/trees pruned
- Yards fertilized twice a year, weed and feed, thatched, aerated: schedule lawn maintenance for the year

Consider adding automotive maintenance:

- Seasonal tires changed out
- Oil/air filter changed, tires rotated (If you use the same dealer, they keep a record of what they have done in the past and the date they did it.)
- Registration due
- Washed/waxed

Finally, you can add personal items:

- Annual doctor appointments: Dentist, Ophthalmologist, Gynecologist, Cardiologist, ENT for hearing aids
- Drivers license renewal

- Passport renewal

- End of year:
    - Clean out files
    - Clean out manuals
    - Gather tax documents before January: donate to get tax deductions by end of year
    - Re-do budget for next year
    - Schedule annual trips

Tips

If you feel overwhelmed because everything is a mess in your house and you don't know where or how to start organizing, go to: www.flylady.net. She has the answers you need, as she is the guru of organization! Her philosophy is easy: do things by zones in your house and take a zone a day. It works!

Keep Busy

"She looketh well to the ways of her household, and eateth not the bread of idleness" (Prov. 31:27).

Reflect on These Questions

CHAPTER 8 QUESTIONS

Home Ownership and Repairs

1. After your husband died, what was the first thing that had to be done to your house?

2. Did your children or a friend help with your house repairs? Did you hire someone or handle them yourself? (If you did them yourself, I applaud you!)

3. Was it necessary for you to move? If so, where and how did you do it?

4. If you gave some things to family members, list them and to whom you gave them. (This might prove helpful later when you can't locate something and don't remember to whom you gave it).

5. Have you ever taken the time to dedicate your home/apartment/motor home or wherever you live, to the Lord? Even if you have lived in it for years, the

Lord would be pleased to hear you pray and ask for His blessing on it. If you did it at one time, when was that? Why not renew it today?

Hold This

"Peace I leave with you, my peace I give unto you: not as the world giveth, give I unto you. Let not your heart be troubled, neither let it be afraid" (John 14:27).

Additional comprehensive questions are provided in chapter eight of:

A Companion Journal,
Good Grief—I Need Relief! A Widow's Guide to
Recovering and Rejoicing.

Chapter Nine

RINGS AND THINGS

To wear or not to wear your wedding band is a huge question to some widows. The decision can be charged with emotion. Some women are inclined to remove it shortly after their husband dies. Other women think that it is betraying their husband if they ever remove it. That is not the case. I wore mine for seven years, as it was my preference.

When people view the ring finger and see a ring there, they assume the woman is married. When a widow decides she is ready to stop wearing her ring, she is simply acknowledging she is no longer married. It doesn't mean that she wants to date, although some might construe it as such.

My ring is significant to me because Warren selected and purchased it while he was stationed in the military in Germany.

The first year after he died, I thought it a shame for my husband's beautiful thick gold wedding band to just lie in a drawer or jewelry box, and decided I would have it made into a pendant.

The jeweler, a designer himself, answered all my questions about using the ring's gold to craft it. I selected the design I liked and he drew a sketch. He assured me that if I wanted to insert the diamond from my band into the center of the heart in the future, then he would make it happen. We clinched the deal after he assured me another double heart-shaped design didn't exist quite like it in my Tri-City area. I couldn't wait for it to be completed.

I picked it up on Valentine's Day, but held off wearing it until the first anniversary of Warren's death, which happened the next month. The Lord allowed me to attend a pastor's school in another state and I was able to see both of my sons there; I wore the necklace for the first time then.

Every time I fastened the chain around my neck, I felt loved. The heart pendant was waiting to clutch my diamond...someday.

As the seventh year of Warren's passing approached, I began to think and pray about exchanging my ring for a Mother's ring, or perhaps putting a gemstone in it. I wrote my children and asked their opinion about placing the diamond into the pendant. They replied that it was fine to do whatever I felt I wanted to do with it.

The anniversary date arrived and I attended GriefShare with a widowed lady in her eighties. After the session, she surprised me with a gracious thank you note which contained a hundred dollar bill. So I took my ring to the jewelers and got an estimate. Since the gift covered all of the expenses, I left my wedding band with him so he could remove the diamond and attach it to my pendant. Two days later, he called to say it was ready. When I picked it up and put it around my neck, it sparkled and seemed to agree with me that it liked its new home. What a blessing that the Lord gives us the desires of our heart, even in ways we hadn't figured.

I am so thankful that the Lord has an open, loving heart just waiting to welcome me when I choose to brush aside the busyness of the world and with a willing heart talk to Him.

Yes, the Lord loves us and He does consider us His jewels. May we give Him our best.

Tip

You can have wedding rings cut in half and made into earrings. Warren had two wedding bands because his first one was thin and when he was at work it was a hazard so I replaced it with a thicker stronger one. When I had my heart necklace designed, I couldn't use the second one which had two toned gold on it, so later I decided to have it made into earrings. I treasure them and I may do the same with my white gold wedding band.

Cherish This

Although there is no biblical reference that directly refers to a "wedding ring," in Bible days, kings used their rings as signatures on official documents. Aren't we blessed that the King of Kings seals us with a seal that can't be broken? According to Jeremiah 31:3, He also loves us with an eternal love, one that never dies, and can't be extinguished.

CAN YOU?

Can you pray the prayer of dedication and mean it from your heart?

PRAYER OF DEDICATION

Lord, we dedicate the rest of our lives to wholly follow You. Thank you for loving and caring for the small things, which loom like mountains before our eyes when we are grieving. Help us to be pleasantly surprised when You give us the peace and wisdom we are searching for in such areas as rings and other things.
In Your precious name, amen.

Reflect on These Questions

CHAPTER 9 QUESTIONS

Rings and Things

1. Did your husband to be ask your dad for permission to marry you before he gave you your ring?

   Tell about it:

2. What is your special story surrounding your ring/rings? (Purchased together, etc.)

3. How long have you worn/or do you plan to wear your rings since becoming a widow?

4. What future plans do you have for them (e.g. store them in a safety deposit box, reset the diamonds into a dinner ring, reset and add some different stones, make it into a necklace or earrings, give as a gift to one of your children)?

5. Do you feel that you need to confer with your family about your plans before you make a final commitment?

Stop and Think

"Is anything too hard for the Lord?..." (Gen. 18:14).

Additional comprehensive questions are provided in chapter nine of:

A Companion Journal,
Good Grief—I Need Relief! A Widow's Guide to
Recovering and Rejoicing.

Chapter Ten

∾ LONELINESS ∾
A KILLER

What exactly is loneliness? To me it is a feeling that overwhelms, engulfs me, and whispers *no one cares about who you are, where you are, and what you do.* It's feeling alone and abandoned.

Although I am not often lonely, it annoys and frustrates me when it happens, because I realize that I am not as close to the Lord as I want to be or should be. My inward thoughts are focused on myself, my desires, and my goals that haven't gone as I wanted or planned.

Loneliness or being by oneself can prove a trial for some people who respond well to the stimulation of being around others. When this need is not fulfilled, it brings sadness.

Many widows complain that the walls seem to close in as sunlight fades to the black of evening and they welcome television and movies as their companions. Since my mom and I like to watch the news at night while we eat our dinner, sometimes we follow that with one of our DVDs, preferring to pick the language and content ourselves rather than taking a chance on whatever might come up on TV. We also enjoy reading and spend a lot of time doing that at night if it's too hot, cold, or windy to go outside and work in the garden or just sit and enjoy the flowers from our patio.

Can loneliness be the reason some widows and widowers don't stay home any more than they have too? Being with people, going places, and keeping busy perhaps keeps them from realizing they are staying away from their house and thinking about other things rather than facing an empty house and perhaps haunting memories.

Loneliness makes having a pet in the home much more appealing to someone who might not travel a lot. Several of our widowed friends have a cat or dog, and thoroughly enjoy them. Mom and I opted out of having a pet. It takes the hassle out of having to find someone to care for them when we want to go out of town to be with family.

My life, however, is filled with caring for the house, yard, cooking, playing the piano, being a companion to my mom, caring for her health issues, working with widows, writing, broadcasting, speaking, and serving in grief ministries.

Oswald Chambers gives his slant on the loneliness issue:

YOU ARE NOT YOUR OWN

"Do you not know that...you are not your own?" (1 Corinthians 6:19).

There is no such thing as a private life, or a place to hide in this world, for a man or woman who is intimately aware of and shares in the sufferings of Jesus Christ. God divides the private life of His saints and makes it a highway for the world on one hand and for Himself on the other. No human being can stand that unless he is identified with Jesus Christ. We are not sanctified for ourselves. We are called into intimacy with the gospel, and things happen that appear to have nothing to do with us. But God is getting us into fellowship with Himself. Let Him have His way. If you refuse, you will be of no value to God in His redemptive work in the world, but will be a hindrance and a stumbling block.

The first thing God does is get us grounded on strong reality and truth. He does this until our cares for ourselves individually have been brought into submission to His way for the purpose of His redemption. Why shouldn't we experience heartbreak? Through those doorways God is opening up ways of fellowship with His

Son. Most of us collapse at the first grip of pain. We sit down at the door of God's purpose and enter a slow death through self-pity. And all the so-called Christian sympathy of others helps us to our deathbed. But God will not. He comes with the grip of the pierced hand of His Son, as if to say, "Enter into fellowship with Me; arise and shine." If God can accomplish His purposes in this world through a broken heart, then why not thank Him for breaking yours? [i]

The What, Where, and When of Loneliness

Here are some widows' responses to questions about loneliness:

When Are You Lonely?

- "Being alone is different than being lonely. I get lonely in the evenings at home. That is the time that I usually chatted or 'shared life' with my husband. I miss that close time together and the oneness that sharing creates."

- "I can get lonely in the midst of a crowd, then I either leave or go home, or if I'm stuck and can't leave, then I just pray. Eventually, I will converse with people around me."

WHERE DO YOU GO?

- "When there is sun, I go outside and enjoy it."
- "I go to my room to be alone."
- "Into my yard and garden to work hard; this helps to chase away the blues."
- "Shopping."
- "Out to eat."
- "To a friend's house."

WHAT DO YOU DO?

- "I reach out and try to find someone who could use an encouraging word, help with their problems, or a helping hand. I like to do good things for others."
- "Invite someone to go somewhere with me (coffee, etc.)."
- "Sometimes I put on a movie that makes me happy, such as a comedy or a cowboy movie."
- "I call a friend, my daughter, or my mom."
- "When I go to my room, I sometimes just get on my knees and pray."
- "I read my Bible (especially the Psalms)."
- "Look at pictures or videos and think about memories the pictures bring back."
- "Do something active with my children."
- "Take a walk."
- "Cook a good meal."

- "Go to church."
- "Clean my house."
- "Try to socialize with someone who could help lift my spirits."
- "Read a Christian book."
- "Anything that will distract my mind and keep me active."
- "I don't feel lonely much, but when I do, I tend to turn toward southern gospel music."
- "I go to Facebook to talk with people."
- "I sit and cuddle my cats."
- "Once in awhile I allow myself time to have a pity party, and I cry and talk to God."
- "I listen to and sing songs that God uses to remind me that He cares."
- "I don't always read the Bible, or listen to Christian music, or pray, but I enjoy getting emails from GriefShare, and save the really good ones and read them over and over."
- "I invite grandkids to sleep over, make crafts, or bake."
- "Sometimes I just lie down and rest."
- "Occasionally I wear my deceased husband's shirt or my dad's."
- "Reading taught me that God desires our love, our heart, our intimacy. He is all we need."

A friend of mine said, "When I'm lonely, I put on music that praises the Lord and picture myself sitting at my Creator's feet just pouring out my heart to Him. Then I start thanking Him. The tears are soon gone and I'm praising Him and rejoicing.

This reminds me of the ten lepers who went to Jesus and asked for healing. He told them to go show themselves to the Priest, which is what they would have done if they had been healed. So, I talk to the Lord, and then act as though I've been healed. Proverbs says to commit your works to the Lord and your thoughts will be established. Somewhere in the process of not acting lonely (for me, that's being cheerful, thankful and singing) the Lord changes my heart and I find that I'm no longer lonely."

The next time you cry, "Lord, do You care? Where are You?" remember He never stops loving us.

Assurance

"I will never leave thee, nor forsake thee" (Heb. 13:5b).

"Draw nigh to God, and He will draw nigh to you," (James 4:8a).

Reflect on These Questions

CHAPTER 10 QUESTIONS

Loneliness

1. Oswald Chambers says we should thank God for our broken heart. Why does he say that?

2. If you live alone, do you have difficulty with loneliness?   When it overcomes you, if you leave the house to get relief where do you like to go and what do you do there?

3. Do you have a pet? What's its name and breed? Did you get it before or after your husband died?

4. Does it travel with you? If not, what arrangements do you make for its care?

5. What has proven effective for you to conquer your loneliness (music, prayer, Bible reading, etc.)?

$\mathcal{V}ictory$

"And the peace of God, which passeth all understanding, shall keep your hearts and minds through Christ Jesus" (Phil. 4:7).

Additional comprehensive questions are provided in chapter ten of:

A Companion Journal,
Good Grief—I Need Relief! A Widow's Guide to Recovering and Rejoicing.

Chapter Eleven

～ EMOTIONS ～
A ROLLER COASTER RIDE

The following paragraphs are extracted thoughts from some journals, which I hope will help you see that although I had struggles, which seemed serious at the time, God also dumped blessings on my life. You might wonder why I included some things in this book, which seem trivial. The answer is that what seems mountainous at the moment, becomes a hill later on. Please think about your own life and how you reacted at the various stages of your grief. Perhaps reading some of my journal entries in different months and even years will help you in some way to realize that you aren't alone, and you will make it by going forward one day at a time by slowing down when you need to, and going forward when you feel stronger.

JUMBLED THOUGHTS FROM MY JOURNALS

"My life seems like a jig-saw puzzle with many pieces missing. The main one in the middle is the largest, Warren and our ministry."

"It also seems that my life has come to a place in a country garden that forks and meanders through life. I don't know which road to take and what ministry to pursue."

"After Warren died, I put off packing things out of his office as long as I could because I dreaded doing it. Why? Because it finalized things, and made me feel like I no longer actually belonged at the church where my husband pastored for seven years. I hated going into our radio station and packing out our CDs for the same reason. It made me realize that neither of us would ever do another broadcast there. Although I have pictures that remind me of the many pleasant hours that were spent in that room, the ache didn't go away by looking at pictures."

"This morning my left leg cramped and I got tangled up in the covers as I desperately tried to get out of bed so I could stand on my foot and stomp on it or simply walk around. In the past when I had extreme cramps so that my leg extended straight out and it was difficult to move, let alone get over the side of the bed, I would yell, 'Help! Warren, push me out of bed, I have a leg cramp!'

"Today I cried out, 'Oh, God, I can't do this!' Then my thoughts drifted to the future when I would still have to push out of bed alone when I had a leg cramp. *What will I do when I became frail?*

"I cried. 'I wish life would simplify—but it's not going to happen.'"

"'Lord, please give me wisdom in the days ahead. I know You will, but my roller coaster emotions are like a bouncing ball. One minute I feel lost, then the next safe, then back into a fog, then happy and sad again...'"

⌒

After I returned to the States, a friend told me, "You are too busy to take time to grieve."

She was right. I think I was involved in too many things and I needed to be silent and feed upon God's Word. Then I could have sorted through things and moved in the right direction more quickly.

⌒

"From the get-go, it was difficult to see happy couples holding hands or sitting together in church. I miss that so much. Warren and I enjoyed sitting together in the front row of church in Japan when someone else preached and he wasn't in the pulpit. We squeezed each other's hands a certain way, a silent signal of our love."

⌒

When someone said, "You need to be assertive and speak up." My reaction was, *I don't feel like being assertive. I just want to be still and let someone else take care of me and figure out the details in this situation. I just can't handle it!*

Acceptance

"Today troubled thoughts descended upon me like the storm clouds that darkened the sky as I stared out my office window. They seemed to frown back as I asked, 'What am I doing here?' *Sometimes I would like to visit my kids and not have these responsibilities.* Then I would catch myself and say, 'Stop it!' and refocus my thoughts above the grizzled clouds. Although I didn't cry today, I felt like it at bedtime."

Enough is Enough!

Dear widowed friend, you will come to a defining stage where you will think or even say, "Enough is enough. I have been stuck in this vicious cycle long enough. Lord, I need to move on. Help me to accept what has happened as reality, what You planned for me, and what You want. Please show me what I need to do in the here and now. I can't linger in the past and what I did or didn't enjoy, or in the future and think about what might have been. Help me, Lord. Show me what I am to do today, and help me accept whatever it is with grace, as from a loving Father's hand."

Less than two months after Warren's death, I wrote: "I feel this morning like I am in a rushing stream that is pulling me away from Warren, and I can't look back and see him. I fling up my arm and try, but I am drug further along; I can't get my breath.

"Most nights I sleep fitfully. Some nights the numbers on my clock stare back at me, as if mocking and daring me to sleep.

"I have trouble remembering what I have said. For instance, 'I will call you,' I said to the real estate agent, and I forgot. Or, I can't recall what time I've made an appointment. Is my sanity on vacation? Will it ever return?

"It feels like I am on a fast merry-go-round and I don't have time to slow down and read anything, except my Bible first thing each morning. Maybe if I slowed down, the reality of mourning might hit me, and I don't want that."

⌒

"You'll make it. It's hard, but you'll make it," my former pastor's widow said to me four months after my husband died. She looked me in the eye and repeated, "You'll make it!" What encouraging words. And later to see her happily remarried and in good spirits, warmed my heart.

⌒

Two months and seven days after Warren died, my brother asked, "How are you doing?" My mind searched for an appropriate answer and "In and out" came out of my mouth before I analyzed why I said it.

"That's a good way to describe it," he replied.

"How am I doing? I just want him to return and give me a hug."

"Yes," my brother said, "Or let us go up there!"

∽

NINTH MONTH

During the Christmas season, I sought a friend at church and my emotions spilled over as I cried, "I need help decorating my plant shelf." Later I felt foolish, but I knew at the time it happened that I needed the emotional release. To cry as I talked seemed to relieve the dam that had built up inside of me.

Nine months after his death: "I still seem to have a lot of brain fog and certain weekdays seem worse than others; usually Sundays are especially hard. I think back on the Sunday routines that we enjoyed in Japan and try to relive them. Sometimes I fixed a crock-pot dinner that was ready to eat when we got home; other times we ate on base with church friends. It was a delight to do either, because we both loved working with the military and the Japanese people."

I felt no one cared when my devotional appeared in a Daily Devotional Guide and was translated into several languages. Warren knew it had been accepted for publication, but never saw it in print. (It appeared nine months after he died). He would have shared my joy.

"This weekend, nine months after he died, I emptied the last two boxes from the family room/office. My bookshelves need rearranging so I can start writing again. I really want to get it done, but an overwhelming feeling attacks me when I think about it. Maybe because it is something I did during a happier time in my life; I'm not sure exactly what it is."

∽

Ten months after his death, I wrote: "I opened a statement from the bank handling our mortgage and noticed the dates didn't make sense. It sent me into a funk as paperwork seemed to inundate me constantly and meant I either had to call the bank or go in and talk to them, and I didn't really want to deal with it either way. It is still hard for me to believe that I am a widow. I felt sad today, and had a headache. The headache is most unusual for me; the sadness comes and goes."

Around that time, a pastor called and said he would drop my support after the year anniversary if I was doing all right. I assured him I was and it would be fine to take on a missionary in my place. He made me promise I would call him if I got in a bind. The call blindsided me.

∽

"It's been eleven months and I miss him so much. I felt his wool shirt in my closet tonight and leaned into it and breathed deeply hoping to smell his cologne. Instead, I smelled my body spray."

∽

At the fourteenth month mark: "Grief makes the sparkle of life retreat."

∽

"I am at the fifteen-month mark and today I wrote a letter to Warren as I wanted to address some unresolved issues that played with my mind. When I had said everything I wanted, then I tore it up and tossed it in the garbage. Only God knows what it said; but it released my unanswered questions and pent-up emotions."

"Today I feel like a limp dishrag when it comes to spiritual things. I feel I am filled with the Holy Spirit as I sing to myself in spiritual songs, but I have no inclination to witness. I feel so bad about it! I don't know if I am trying to rely upon others, or just what. I used to love to go door-to-door and witness; but I don't really love it anymore. I feel terrible that I feel this way, but I can't seem to move forward."

∽

"It's been sixteen months since Warren passed away and I still have moments, even days, when I feel very lonely."

∽

"I owed a late fee for my income tax, and wondered if I would be penalized for getting Medicare RX late due to the fact that I lived out of country and had other insurance there. The issue resolved in my benefit. Thank you so much, dear Lord!"

∾

"The ache for him is so deep today. I just want him to step out of the picture on my dresser and let me lean against him and have him put his arms around me and squeeze me."

∾

"It has been sixteen months since Warren passed away. I love it when I sit on the back patio and hear the birds twittering during a short lull in the traffic. I also love the fresh smells in the early morning after the sprinklers have come on and the drops of water paint the plants with crystal dew."

TRIGGER MOMENTS

"Of course I still have moments, even days, when I feel very lonely. I also have 'trigger moments' when I am in a store as I was this week in Costco and I flashed back to being with Warren at Costco in Japan. Although the trip through congested traffic wearied me, it always revived and revitalized me when we arrived at the Costco in Japan. It was a pleasure to once again enjoy a taste of America while living far from the States.

"Once as we traveled to Costco, Warren cut off a trucker and didn't blink his lights to indicate he was sorry or to say, 'thank you' because we didn't know that was culturally expected. The driver kept forcing us closer and closer to a railing and almost made us crash. That's when Warren decided my small car was not safe for me to drive, and he traded it in.

"Sometimes these 'trigger moments' are pleasant; most of the time they make me sad because I will never be able to return and experience my former life again."

⮌

"Sunday, February 14, twenty-three months have passed and I was finally able to thank the Lord for being a widow and for the various ministries I have."

SECOND ANNIVERSARY

"Warren has been gone two years today. It's hard to believe. I am hurting because I lost the beautiful heart necklace pendant that I had made from his wedding ring. I can't replace it. (I later located it!) I wonder what he is doing in heaven and feel like I am a failure here on earth. I have tried to stay extra busy, but in the back of my mind, I remain sad."

BLESSINGS

As I read through my journals, I stopped to consider the blessings that the Lord gave me. Although I had enjoyed each thing, I didn't always realize them for the blessings they were. Give journaling a chance and you will discover what I mean. Here are a few blessings that I rediscovered:

1. A yellow butterfly came into my yard, not the mundane everyday white Cabbage Butterfly.

2. My out-of-state brother-in-law came and put together our porch swing.

3. While I sat on the porch swing on my patio having my devotions, a hummingbird lit on a purple petunia.

4. KaraTek (ktekint.org) took *Rejoicing With Joyce International* on as a project.

5. I asked the Lord for a sign (oh ye of little faith!) about whether I was actually supposed to produce *Rejoicing with Joyce* devotions on the radio and He answered my prayer in an unusual way. While I attended the fiftieth wedding anniversary of long-time friends, someone talked to me about it, and recommended it to some friends.

6. A church friend asked me to ride with her out of state so I could visit my son and his family.

7. My mother is still going strong although she's in her nineties.

8. I prayed to get to know the teens at church better, and the opportunity opened to play the piano for a small teen ensemble.

9. I drove to see my brother without getting sleepy (approximately 150 miles). That might seem

ridiculous to you, but it seemed like a long ways to me.

10. Had a melt-in-your-mouth huckleberry scone and tea at a Victorian House with ladies in my family. I purchased *The Tea Lover's Devotional* by Emilie Barnes, and some strawberry tea. Delightful.

11. At a thrift store, I found a long skirt for our church's annual Old Fashioned Day.

12. While at a writer's conference in another town, I met a Christian writer from my area.

13. I enjoyed communing with the Lord as the chilly early morning air (in the 50s) and the chirping of birds refreshed me on the balcony of my brother's home right after the sun rose and kissed my face.

14. I love unexpected pleasures. A dear friend called me this evening from another state, and we shared pleasant memories for thirty minutes. It was so sweet; it made my day.

A fact: "Death short-circuited my thought processes and everyday things became difficult to manage. I felt like my brain had been painted with fuzz."

As time passed, I found it easier to cope with ordinary problems, and I could again read the Bible and pray. Although at times I found it difficult to stay close to the Lord, He never strayed from me.

"Have pity upon me, have pity upon me, O ye my friends; for the hand of God hath touched me" (Job 19:21).

Blessings

"Blessed be the Lord, who daily loadeth us with benefits, even the God of our salvation" (Ps. 68:19).

Encouragement

"But He knoweth the way that I take: when He hath tried me, I shall come forth as gold" (Job 23:10).

Reflect on These Questions

CHAPTER 11 QUESTIONS

Emotions

1. Have you had an emotional flashback? If so, where were you? What "triggered" the moment?

2. Do you feel like you can't go on alone? Explain why.

3. Are you involved in some worthwhile things or are you hiding in your house hating to face the day?

4. What in particular seems to be overwhelming (repairs, paperwork, etc.)?

5. If you kept a journal, share some of your important thoughts on your road to recovery.

If you have never kept one, why not buy a journal, notebook, or tablet (anything will work, it doesn't have to be expensive), and start tracking your journey by writing down your feelings either by the day, or the week? You will be amazed when you look back in future years and relive some incidents you might have forgotten.

Overwhelmed?

"Hear my cry, O God; attend unto my prayer. From the end of the earth will I cry unto thee, when my heart is overwhelmed: lead me to the rock that is higher than I. For thou hast been a shelter for me, and a strong tower from the enemy.
I will abide in thy tabernacle for ever:
I will trust in the covert of thy wings. Selah" (Ps. 61:1-4).

Additional comprehensive questions are provided in chapter eleven of:

A Companion Journal,
Good Grief—I Need Relief! A Widow's Guide to
Recovering and Rejoicing.

Chapter Twelve

∽ HOLIDAYS & ANNIVERSARIES ∽ COPING WITHOUT RETREATING TO A DESERT ISLAND!

The first time a holiday and our anniversary came around, it was tough. I wanted everything to be as it was the year before in Japan, but it was so different and never could be the same. No one around me could step into my current world or visualize the world I had left, or imagine how I felt about both of them.

ANNIVERSARIES

If we were in Japan during our anniversary, we drove through congested traffic to another town until we saw the building housing the Outback Restaurant. I loved, and usually enjoyed, Alice Springs Chicken. My husband kept teasing me about going to a steak house and eating chicken till I finally gave in and started enjoying their petite steaks.

Our special fiftieth anniversary rolled around three years after Warren graduated to heaven. I decided that year instead of purchasing the traditional piece of jewelry, which he usually gave me, I would buy something that I could see and enjoy every day and not something that remained hidden in a jewelry box most of the time.

I visited some nurseries and ended up with a black wrought iron hanging basket holder. It sits on my patio and holds the plants or flowers of my choice; it continues to bring me pleasure from year to year.

THANKSGIVING

If I jumped onto the nostalgic shelf, and burrowed into the last Thanksgiving my husband and I shared together, I would remember it was spent with the dear people at the church my husband pastored in Japan. The food signup sheet always filled up quickly as people chose whether to bake pies or smoke a turkey or ham.

The moment one walked into the room where we met for dinner, the festive holiday decorations welcomed us, and the aroma of the special occasion enveloped us. Even the tables seemed to approve as the food prepared with love piled on them. The fellowship of kindred spirits encouraged lasting friendships.

After the meal, we moved to the main auditorium for a time of thanksgiving and testimonies. We shared how the Lord had blessed each of us with special, varied pleasures throughout the year. Then a lot of hands helped clean up the dining area so the room would be ready for the children's meeting the next evening.

When good-byes were said, several single airmen and some women usually accompanied us home. After a nap, they all helped us set up and decorate our Christmas tree, and then we shared snacks and parted with special memories stored in our hearts.

CHRISTMAS BEFORE

Christmas in Japan included a lot of music. There was always a time of singing carols at the train station, and at the food court on base, an adult choir cantata at our church, a ladies progressive dinner, and an adult Christmas Banquet. Special tickets were printed and given out to invite not only military people to the holiday functions, but also the dear Japanese people. Translation into Japanese was provided for our cantata.

Our caroling time at the train station included some of our church people handing out special packs prepared with tissue packets, candy, and a gospel tract inside them. People seemed more receptive to accepting the packets if they were handed to them by children. Children are held in high regard in Japan because most families are small.

Some church members brought musical instruments and played them while others enjoyed singing the hymns. We usually had some visitors at church as a result. The hearts of both members and visitors were blessed as a result of these efforts.

⌒

I remember a special Christmas, one I looked forward to with great anticipation. I was to play the piano for some families from our church while they sang Christmas carols at a Japanese nursing home. I never anticipated the joy that would accompany that extraordinary Christmas experience.

Although we did not know beforehand that the facility where we were going housed the poorer people in Japan, it really didn't matter. That is where I discovered wealth—in the midst of seniors reduced in circumstances.

We signed up in advance to attend the Christmas carol singing because the Japanese, meticulous and professional in details, not only anticipated our program, but they also planned who would greet us, who would show us where to park, how many people they would serve refreshments to, and numerous other behind the scene details, such as how many slippers they needed to provide for our group.

Twenty children and adults from our church piled into vans and drove the winding streets of Tokyo that nippy day. Greeters met us in front of the nursing home and pointed us around the building to the backside. Other

Japanese people waited to show us a no parking area, and then placed signs on our windshields saying we had permission to park there. Extreme shortage of parking in Tokyo made these drastic measures necessary.

We removed our shoes inside the door as custom dictated. A Japanese woman then welcomed us and handed us hot green tea from her tray. The warmth of the tea contrasted the starkness of the room. No beautifully colored carpet, drapes, pictures, or gilded mirrors greeted us as we walked into the room. There were tall windows on two sides of the large room. The cold floors made us thankful for our slippers.

The stage, erected for our program, held a whimsical tree decorated in traditional Asian colors of orange and yellow. It was the only note of Christmas that was apparent, because Christmas is not usually celebrated in Japan. Microphones waited in the middle of the stage.

The sea of senior Japanese faces lit up as the children climbed the steps to the platform.

"Thank you for allowing us to come today," our leader said, and then announced each song in English interspersed with the true meaning of Christmas. "God, the Creator of the universe, sent His only Son, Jesus Christ, from heaven as a gift to all who will receive Him. He died and rose again to pay for our sins. He is the real reason that we celebrate Christmas."

As the program progressed, the children on stage grew restless. The younger ones sat down on the platform, but continued to sing. The Japanese nodded their heads in time to the Christmas carols, softly clapped, or attempted to mouth the words. A few tried to sing, or direct the songs with their hands in the air. Most just sat absorbed in the moment, perhaps remembering happier years when their homes rang with the laughter of children.

The gospel message was new to most. The penetrating thoughts translated into Japanese kept nearly everyone awake during the entire program. One woman nodded in agreement, as if she truly understood that Christ offered her the best Christmas gift, one filled with love, purchased just for her.

The Japanese men and women clapped heartily at the end. The children paired up and took baskets of candy to the audience seated at the tables. Eyes gleamed as hands reached out to touch the children.

"Candy for you," a little curly headed girl said as she held out an individually wrapped piece of chocolate.

"Oh, thank you," the seniors responded in Japanese. No one refused. People in Japan adore children. Perhaps it's because most families have only one or two children; their homes or apartments are tiny and their country is crowded.

I followed after the little ones, shook hands, spoke a short Japanese phrase (my entire repertoire), and thanked them for attending our program.

A mature-faced man looked up at me as I offered him my hand. He smiled as tears of joy rolled down his wrinkled face and he pointed to his open Bible and said, "I Christian!"

I bent down to be sure that I had heard him correctly. He repeated, "I Christian."

I was elated. "That is wonderful that you are a Christian. I am a Christian too! One day we will live in heaven," I said and pointed skyward.

He nodded his head and said, "She Christian too," indicating the woman seated next to him. I greeted her with a bow, spoke with her a moment, and then continued shaking hands.

I rejoiced and felt humbled that the Lord had allowed me to meet these special people.

Statistics estimate about one-half of one percent of the Japanese claim to be Christians. What are the chances of meeting one Christian? Yet the Lord allowed me to meet a Christian Japanese married couple, living in a nursing home in Tokyo, Japan.

What a rare find! I felt I had been handed a special Christmas gift.

We thanked the nursing home for letting us come as much as they thanked us for coming. As our families gathered to leave, each person received a handmade Christmas card with Merry Christmas written on the outside, and a Japanese greeting on the inside. Someone had spent hours folding tiny origami figures and inserting them with love inside those cards.

With joyful hearts, we loaded into our vans. What a wonderful way for families to spend a day in the Christmas season—sharing the love of Christ with others.

There are thousands of seniors in nursing homes throughout the world just waiting for someone to give them a rare gift—the true Christmas story!

How My Life Changed

My life now is shared with my extended family. We get together for major holidays and enjoy each other's company around a table laden with great food. New traditions have been instigated such as going around the table and telling a highlight from the previous year, or some way the Lord has blessed us in the current year.

Christmas Now

Why dread the holidays? This Christmas can be different and exciting!

My first year as a widow found me frustrated because I couldn't locate my tree decorations. I finally gave up and purchased some inexpensive ones.

Later it occurred to me why I couldn't find the old ones, even though I prayed a lot about them. The Lord didn't want me sitting and staring at the tree with sad memories pricking me as I reminisced through past years when Warren and I always snuggled and enjoyed the lights together. For seven years we enjoyed Christmas activities with our church family in Japan. Although we missed our children and friends in the States, in our hearts we knew we were in God's will and where He wanted us.

This year, however, He wanted me to enjoy a new color theme, sparkly lights with quiet music playing in the background, and my favorite holiday candle wafting cinnamon scent everywhere.

The years have flown by since Warren graduated to heaven. Now, Mom and I enjoy Christmas in our new home. I love to decorate right after Thanksgiving. We prepare our hearts and minds for the coming holiday which helps us move past enduring it to anticipating the time our family from out of town will spend with us, a great meal, a gift exchange, and a special time of Christmas carol singing. We also look forward to greeting friends we haven't seen for awhile, as well as the special ones that we enjoy frequently.

PRACTICAL WAYS TO BLESS OTHERS AT CHRISTMAS

- Purchase a poinsettia in honor of your husband, and donate it to your church as a decoration during the Christmas holiday.
- Honor him with a day sponsorship to a Christian radio station.
- Purchase a gift that your husband would have liked, and donate it to a pastor or missionary who could use it in his ministry.
- Pause and think of the less fortunate throughout your city, state, country, and the world; pray for them and count your blessings.
- Send a donation through your church to a ministry that assists widows in other countries.

SEND SOME FRESH ENCOURAGEMENT TO A WIDOW

- Invite another widow to help you bake some things she can give as gifts to friends and family such as breads, cookies, candy, some roasted pecans, or simple crafts. The fellowship will bless you both.
- Make a holiday wreath for each of your front doors.
- Shop together for supplies to assemble a handcraft for some underprivileged children.
- Invite her to help you decorate your tree and/or home. The next day, decorate hers.

- Help each other put up your outside lights (enlist a teen if needed).

- Put her name on the Christmas caroling list at your church if she attends somewhere else.

- Sometime in December, volunteer together to help serve a meal at a local mission.

- Take her on a short sightseeing trip to view Christmas lights, then stop and purchase an ornament for your trees as a keepsake. End with coffee or tea and later purchase her favorite flavor as a gift.

- Make some gift baskets together for other widows or some nursing home shut-ins who have no one coming to visit them during the holidays. Enjoy delivering them together.

- If she doesn't have family in the area, invite her to your house for Christmas dinner. She might even like to come early and help with the meal preparation.

- Make her a tree ornament with her husband's name on it with gold or silver glitter. Give her small pieces of colored paper to match so she can write special memories to put inside the ornament.

Increase your joy this season by relaxing, pondering, and letting go of the hassle which can overwhelm us as it pushes for perfection in everything related to the holidays.

Dear widow, you are loved! Please enjoy the Christmas season.

Take Heart

"The LORD relieveth the fatherless and widow..."
(Ps. 146:9b).

Reflect on These Questions

CHAPTER 12 QUESTIONS

Holidays and Anniversaries

1. Which holidays and holiday traditions stand out to you?

2. Do you still celebrate them in the same way you did with your husband? If not, how have they changed?

3. What outstanding memory do you have of Christmas?

4. How would you change the memories that you have of your holidays if you could go back and revisit them?

5. What special things did you traditionally do with your husband on your anniversary?

Our Strength

"The LORD upholdeth all that fall, and raiseth up all those that be bowed down" (Ps. 145:14).

Additional comprehensive questions are provided in chapter twelve of

A Companion Journal,
Good Grief—I Need Relief! A Widow's Guide to
Recovering and Rejoicing.

PART THREE

Looking Forward

"The steps of a good man are ordered by the LORD: and he delighteth in his way"
(Ps. 37:23).

Chapter Thirteen

∽ DATING AND REMARRIAGE ∽ WHAT'S THIS?

To date, or not to date? Most widows don't even want to hear or think about such a thing, especially immediately after burying their husband. And rightly so. Later down the road, however, there might come a time when that thought enters your mind, particularly if you are alone a lot, and the walls seem to close in and there is no one to share your heart with.

One day I opened an email from a dear friend in Japan. She said, "If you meet a nice man, I feel sure that Warren would think it was all right for you to get remarried, even if he didn't say so before he passed away."

It made me sad; I bowed my head. Tears fell.

I appreciated her thoughtfulness and responded, "I have asked the Lord to give me a ministry if He didn't have another husband for me. I will be fine." And I was.

My brother encouraged me to try online dating, which worked well for him. He even said he would pay my fee for one year. I filled out the form and tried the free trial for a week, but the man that I wrote didn't respond, so I decided I didn't have the time or patience to continue to work the system, and closed down my information.

I didn't actually date for about four years, and then only once with someone in full-time ministry. We both agreed it wasn't the Lord's will for us.

Now, after six years, the Lord has graciously given me enjoyment, peace, and contentment as the primary caregiver for my aging mother; being involved with the widows in our church; our bereavement outreach, GriefShare; my family; writing and producing my devotional radio broadcast *RejoicewithJoyce.org*; working with children; and gardening. I have taken to heart Psalm 104:35, "My meditation of him shall be sweet: I will be glad in the LORD."

If you are of another persuasion and feel that you want or need to get remarried, I would love to share some thoughts with you. These are based on observations I have made through the years while being in full-time ministry and since then as a widow.

Some men can talk the talk, but don't walk the walk. They might agree to attend church with you, but that might be as deep as their spirituality goes. Some questions to ponder and find answers too:

- What's his church background?
- Is he a Christian? (Don't take yes as an answer. Delve deeper to find out why he considers himself to be one and how he came to that conclusion. Does he believe it is only by faith through the blood of the Lord Jesus Christ, or do works, church membership, and baptism also play a part?)
- How important is his Bible to him? Check it out and see how long he's had it. Does he use it daily?
- Do you share prayer requests with ease and then pray together?
- Observe his interaction with other people. Does he have to be the center of attention? Is he loud, rude, and demanding, or, quiet and courteous, or just fun and easy to be around, etc.?
- Are people drawn to him or do they shy away?
- Where does he like to hang out?
- What does he do for recreation?
- Is his financial life stable, or is he in debt? Does he try to borrow money from you or his family? Does he gamble?
- Is he divorced, a widower, or never married?
- Does he work or is he retired?
- How does your family feel about him? Have you met his family? If so, do you interact well with each other's family?

- If you have children in the home, how does he get along with them? They with him? If he has children, will they get along with yours?
- Have you asked your pastor's take on the situation? What was his counsel?

May the Lord give you discernment and peace about your relationship if it is meant to be; He will faithfully guide you.

A widow shares her thoughts: "I knew that I wanted to remarry because I didn't want to be alone forever. Two years later, friends introduced me to a man. The Lord gave us both the same scripture, 'He healeth the broken hearted.' The rest is history, and we have been happily married for several years."

Be Assured

"Whoso findeth a wife findeth a good thing, and obtaineth favour of the LORD" (Prov. 18:22).

Comfort

"And the LORD, he it is that doth go before thee; he will be with thee, he will not fail thee, neither forsake thee: fear not, neither be dismayed" (Deut. 31:8).

Reflect on These Questions

CHAPTER 13 QUESTIONS

Dating and Remarriage

1. Thoughts you might like to share with your family members to let them know how you feel about dating and remarriage include:

2. How do you feel about the suggestions that people have given you regarding a future husband?

3. How long after your husband's death would you think you might be ready to date?

4. Where did you or could you find an eligible man (online, at church, social function, former friend, etc.)?

5. What qualities do you want to see in a second husband?

Released

"For the woman which hath an husband is bound by the law to her husband so long as he liveth; but if the husband be dead, she is loosed from the law of her husband" (Rom. 7:2).

Additional comprehensive questions are provided in chapter thirteen of:

A Companion Journal,
Good Grief—I Need Relief! A Widow's Guide to Recovering and Rejoicing.

Chapter Fourteen

⤳ MISSING INGREDIENTS ⤳
THE SEARCH IS ON

*J*ust like certain ingredients are necessary for making a cake turn from a cup of flour to a delicious two layer delight, there are some things that married couples enjoy that make singles wistful.

Several of those things are now missing from my life and its Box of Marriage Memories. However, their memories are tucked into my mind where I can bring them out and reminisce. Things which once brought sparkle to my eyes and zest to my life include some of the following, but are not limited to this list:

- His kiss on my nose
- The crook of his arm
- Holding hands
- The love light in his eyes
- Feeling secure and protected
- Sharing memories

- Being categorized as a couple was a total privilege that many feel frivolous about
- My cold feet on his warm ones
- Eating out together
- Buying him presents and he for me
- Intimacy
- Sharing burdens
- Traveling together by car
- Flying to and from Japan
- Christmas in a foreign land
- The challenges of parking for a progressive dinner for ladies in Japan
- Short furloughs
- Dressing to please him
- Him listening to my problems and wanting to fix them
- Praying together
- Reading his thoughts
- Ministering together and assisting at the altar
- Relaxing together after the evening service
- Military and missionary guests in our home
- Singing together for years
- Accompanying his vocal solos on the piano
- Hearing him play brass instruments well
- Seeing his zeal and love for people
- His Mensa mind (he had a great memory!)

- His help in locating lost items such as my glasses
- Relaxing with him chauffeuring me, especially on long trips
- His spell checking for me
- Warren loved people and he could talk to anyone about sports. While we were seated in an airport in Japan, he recognized a retired sports figure from the United States and walked over, learned he was a Christian, engaged him in conversation, and got his autograph.
- He also excelled in facts about the Civil War, and enjoyed visiting various battlefields. If we didn't have guests in our home, he usually retired early and read in bed. He shifted between Christian books or his favorite fiction writer, Louis L'Amour. He had a large collection of his paperbacks and told me he had read everything L'Amour had written.
- Since we didn't speak Japanese, we didn't subscribe to their TV channels. So we either purchased movies online or when we came to the States we bought family DVDs, war movies, and westerns that included his favorite character, John Wayne.
- Warren made people feel special by taking a personal interest in them. When someone visited our church and returned several months later, he could call them by name. He enjoyed meeting newcomers to the church, and then visiting with them in their home to learn more about them. He always looked for an opportunity to present the gospel.

- He did not like to lose in any type of sport. Before he went into the ministry, he bowled on several teams. When Nintendo put out the Wii, we purchased it in Japan. He had perfected the bowling game with his right hand, so he switched to his left.

- When he preached, he expected someone to get saved and was disappointed if no one responded to the gospel. The Lord gifted him in giving an invitation that touched hearts. The last night he preached, he was discouraged because there was not a salvation decision that day, so I invited a young airman over to our house after the evening service so they could fellowship. They enjoyed playing the Wii together. My regret is that I didn't obey the prompting of the Holy Spirit and also invite another couple who I felt He wanted me to ask. Warren played the Wii the Monday morning that he died.

- Warren used his strong high tenor voice for the glory of the Lord all of his life. He had a desire to record a CD, but never had the opportunity to fulfill that wish. He also loved southern gospel music.

A STAGE

As I looked through one of my photo albums, it dawned on me that no one on this earth knew exactly the same people, and had had the same experiences with me, except Warren. It depressed me to think that link to the past no longer existed, and never would again. It gripped my heart, and squeezed it hard enough so that tears flowed. What about all the happy times when we were teens, or in Bible College going through hard times? And so on. I could talk about them with a friend, and they might nod their head, but there would be no way a kindred spirit could be ignited.

Viewing it now, a few years later, it doesn't bother me, but it was an experience the size of a dark thundercloud when I had it.

One day I sat down and wrote in the front of one of my journals a list of the different places we lived and noted the years we lived there. It put my life into a timeline and a perspective of how many times we had moved. In the future I can refer back to it should my memory deteriorate, or if I need to jog my memory about what years I knew a certain person.

I have stored papers and memorabilia in a plastic bin in my garage. I also have kept cards and photos that I have received through the years from people in our church family at Yokota in the scrapbook that the ladies made for me there. I can see the growth in their children through the years.

PRESERVING MEMORIES

Widows, where are you keeping your husband's special things that you don't want to part with? Do you have a designated area in your closet or on a shelf somewhere in your house? How about a suitcase?

*H*int

Make a scrap memorial book with special folders, flyers, or souvenirs that remind you of favorite times together during your marriage. It might include places you visited on vacations, famous landmarks, concert programs, etc. This can be passed on to your family along with your journal.

A WIDOW'S SAGE ADVICE:

"Let go of the past, keep the memories, and go forward. After awhile, you should move on and enjoy every season of your life." –Angelina, a senior widow

A Word to the Wise

"Heaviness in the heart of man maketh it stoop: but a good word maketh it glad" (Prov. 12:25).

Reflect on These Questions

CHAPTER 14 QUESTIONS

Missing Ingredients

1. Dear widow, what ingredients are missing in your life that gave you a savory past? Post your special list here:

2. What ten things did you love most about your husband?

3. What positive traits best describe your husband that you would like to share with your future generations?

4. Do the same steps for yourself.

5. He and I excelled in different ways. He liked to:

   But I enjoyed:

Commit to It

"The LORD also will be a refuge for the oppressed, a refuge in times of trouble" (Ps. 9:9).

Additional comprehensive questions are provided in chapter fourteen of

A Companion Journal,
Good Grief—I Need Relief! A Widow's Guide to
Recovering and Rejoicing.

Chapter Fifteen

SCRIPTURAL PROMISES FOR WIDOWS

*H*ave you heard it said, "The Bible says a lot of good things that benefit widows"? I heard that saying many times and one day I decided to search it out to see if it was so. I studied every verse that mentioned the word widow, widows, and widowhood. Here are some. See if you agree—God loves and cares for widows.

1. A widow is not to be afflicted, and if she cries out to the Lord, He will hear! (Ex. 22:22-23).

2. In Bible days when a woman became a widow, it was customary for her to return to her childhood home if she had no children. She waited there for a brother-in-law to get old enough to marry her to carry on the family name (Gen. 38:11). Perhaps it was also for her to be able to enjoy the safety of family and get away from the stigma of widowhood (Lev. 22:13).

3. Vows of widows were to be kept. They were to stand and be fulfilled, because she had no husband to disannul them (Num. 30:9).

4. The Lord executes judgment for the fatherless and widows and promises to give them food and clothing (Deut. 10:18).

5. Widows were included every three years in the "Poor tithe" or the "Third tithe" which helped the needy (Deut. 14:29, 26:12).

6. Widows were to rejoice (with their families) before the Lord where He chose, and also during feasts (Deut. 16:11, 14).

7. Widows were not to be lazy, but were to glean in the harvest fields. The Lord promised to bless the work of the hands of farmers if they helped widows, strangers, and the fatherless (Deut. 24:19).

8. The farmers weren't to go over their crops twice, but widows were encouraged to gather olives for oil, and grapes for drinks and eating (Deut. 24:20, 21).

9. There was a curse on anyone who turned aside a judgment for a widow (Deut. 27:19).

10. A widow was blessed who obeyed God's prophet when he told her to make a little cake for him first because the "Lord God of Israel says, The barrel of meal shall not waste, neither shall the cruse of oil

fail, until the day that the Lord sendeth rain upon the earth" (1 Kings 17:14).

Notice:

- She gave Elijah water; he gave her hope.

- She listened to the man of God's request, and obeyed in faith. God used the widow to sustain Elijah and Elijah to sustain the widow.

- The Lord kept His word and she fed Elijah and her family for many days.

- She blessed him by allowing him to stay in her loft.

- When her son died, she immediately talked to Elijah, and he blessed her again by raising him (through the power of the Lord) from the dead (1 Kings 17:22-23).

11. "The LORD preserves the strangers; he relieves the fatherless and widow" (Ps. 146:9).

12. Need help? "For he shall deliver the needy when he crieth; the poor also, and him that hath no helper" (Ps. 72:12). Widows are needy and have lost their helper!

13. The LORD establishes the border of the widow (Prov. 15:25).

14. God's people are commanded to learn to do well; seek justice, relieve the oppressed, bring justice to the fatherless, and plead for the widow (Isa. 1:17).

15. The LORD will judge those who swear falsely against or oppress the widow and fatherless and don't fear Him (Mal. 3:5).

He Sustains

"God is my strength and power: and He maketh my way perfect" (2 Sam. 22:33).

Reflect on These Questions

CHAPTER 15 QUESTIONS

Scriptural Promises for Widows

1. How many of these promises have you claimed?

2. Which one blessed you the most?

3. What have you shared with a friend, family member, or widow about how much God loves widows?

4. After listening to a widow's particular problem, have you shared one of the verses with her? Which one brought her comfort?

5. What two things does the Lord promise to give the fatherless and widows in (Deut. 10:18)?

A Caring Widow

"Cause me to hear thy lovingkindness in the morning; for in thee do I trust: cause me to know the way wherein I should walk; for I lift up my soul unto thee" (Ps. 143:8).

Additional comprehensive questions are provided in chapter fifteen of:

A Companion Journal,
Good Grief—I Need Relief! A Widow's Guide to Recovering and Rejoicing.

Chapter Sixteen

FINANCIAL TIPS
FOR SURVIVING WIDOWHOOD

*A*fter my missionary husband's massive heart attack and memorial service in Tokyo, I moved back to the States and settled in the Pacific Northwest.

My brother, Glenn, became my financial advisor. After working with my incoming and outgoing figures, he announced, "You are going to have to get a job!" That was unwelcomed news since my past several years had been given to full-time ministry, with more experience than pay. I was bewildered in what direction to turn to find a job. Besides, most companies hired younger women who were savvy with the latest electronics that I had no clue about. (Remember that we left for Japan when most people retired!) Although I didn't need a lot of money, a steady income would be a plus.

However, I worried needlessly. The Lord brought the job to me as He soon opened a part-time job in the missions department of my sending church, where I knew the staff and felt at ease. The couple that trained me were personal friends and had actually come to Japan and installed a live-streaming radio station at the church my husband pastored. The salary met my needs and had a bonus—I got to correspond with the several hundred missionaries our church supported. I was the first to read the letters we received weekly. What a joy to be involved in the missions' conference each year and to help coordinate it. Yes, the Lord had it planned and tailor-made.

How about you? Are you—as a lot of widows—suddenly faced with fewer funds and lots of bills? What can you do? What will happen if you have an emergency? Or what if you simply can't pay a bill?

- **First** – Don't panic!

- **Second** – Determine your monthly set financial commitments.

- **Third** – Prepare for the future as much as possible.

- **Fourth** – Look around you.

- **Fifth** – Look up.

FIRST – DON'T PANIC!

Panic is counterproductive! Grieving is natural and necessary, but along with that comes the need for action. It might be a good idea to seek clear-headed advice from your pastor, a financial advisor, or another widow—or maybe all of these.

After the funeral, my mission's representative had a talk with my family and me and told us their policy. I needed to write a letter and ask the churches that had supported Warren and me to please continue for a year while I got settled; then they were no longer under any obligation to continue financial support.

During that year, I found it helpful to counsel with a life insurance financial advisor. I also sought counsel from other widows in our church. We had common problems and concerns about the future. Thankfully, they had traveled the road longer than I, and gave me help. One assured me that "the Lord had something special for you to do." Another friend encouraged me by coming over several days a week and helping me get the neglected yard work done around the repo house that my mom and I purchased.

I was encouraged when I talked to my pastor because he lost his wife about the same time I lost my husband. He had an understanding heart and gave me the opportunity for a fulfilling ministry in the missions department.

When the year passed, I found it difficult to write a follow-up letter because I felt the tether loosened and wondered what the future held without that support each month. Here is an excerpt from my letter:

"He that dwelleth in the secret place of the most High shall abide under the shadow of the Almighty" (Ps. 91:1).

Dear Pastors and Church Friends,

I think widows might cherish this verse because seclusion seems to bring security from the world.

Frankly that is the way I felt when Warren's "Mission Accomplished" happened last March 17th, and he graduated to heaven without me. I just wanted peace and quietness—a retreat if you please.

So my eighty-nine-year-old mother and I purchased a repo-home that we knew was a gift from the Lord.

Warren took such good care of me that I had difficulty pumping gas for the first time when I returned to the States. (They pump it for you in Japan!) There have been many firsts for me including: Moving back from a foreign country, going through numerous boxes of books and other household goods that had been stored for seven years, joining a church by myself, assembling furniture, learning to handle outdoor responsibilities (I still don't have that one down!), driving out of town (I consider long distance anything over an hour's drive), and many other numerous tasks.

I thank you loyal prayer warriors and givers for upholding me during so many days, weeks, and even months of unclear thinking. I realize that only widows and widowers can verify the feeling, but God has been my constant companion, for which I am most grateful.

Some have asked how and what I am doing. With God's help—and my mother claiming she is raising me for the second time—I am doing well.

Since Warren and I didn't own any property or a house, I was unsure where to relocate. After praying (and thank you to those who joined me), the Lord allowed me to return to our sending church, Riverview Baptist in Pasco, Washington. Pastor Paisley graciously offered me the job of Missions Secretary when the position opened. It has been a blessing to still be in touch with over 360 missionaries that the church supports.

Other opportunities the Lord has allowed me to be involved in include: helping start a fellowship for widows called "Help-Hers." We address practical needs such as finances, gardening, making a will, health issues, and of course, encouraging each other through spiritual problems. I pray this will become a real outreach to meet lost widows and lead them to the Lord. It seems to be uncharted water in a lot of churches.

After school on Fridays, I drove to a government school and assisted in one of our several Bible Clubs. There have been hundreds saved through this ministry, what a privilege and a blessing!

This summer I hope to hold a Neighborhood Bible Club for the children around me. Some of them attended the after-school Good News Clubs and told me they got saved there. Please pray that the other lost children in my area and their parents will get saved this summer.

As I continue the next phase of my life, I covet your prayers. May God use you and me to bless many.

Would you prayerfully consider the BIMI military ministry, when you take on another missionary in my place? It was Warren's heartthrob.

Until we rejoice together around the throne, I remain His servant,

Joyce Webster

SECOND – DETERMINE YOUR MONTHLY SET FINANCIAL COMMITMENTS.

What expenses cannot be eliminated: utilities, food, gas, medical expenses, perhaps car payments or a mortgage, etc.? After a couple of years of not budgeting, the time came for the necessity of carefully watching what I spent. If you haven't handled the finances in your home in the past, as I hadn't, find someone to help you set up a budget, and determine to stick to it. Frugal becomes the byword.

Yes, frugal becomes the byword, and perhaps a new normal. Automatic payments may be of benefit; then you don't have to worry about when to pay something. Check your first bank statement to be sure the auto thing really happened. If it's not there, and it should have been according to the date, call right away to check on it. Beware of late fees!

Perhaps you have always done online banking or written out the checks and you are on top of what needs to be paid when and where. If so, good for you.

THIRD – PREPARE FOR THE FUTURE AS MUCH AS POSSIBLE.

How about the future? Do you have an emergency fund available? If not, do give some thought to it.

After Warren died, I called my brother and said, "I don't know what to do about this CD that is maturing."

He said, "Call around to some banks and ask what their current rates are, and reinvest with the best rate."

"I can't do that," I replied. "I just can't bring myself to do that. It overwhelms me!" Since he had lost his wife before I lost my husband, I was sure he would understand. He didn't. He and his company had dealt with investments for many years and it was no big deal to him.

"Yes, you can. It's just everyday life." I tried to argue, but he would have none of it. I called some other widows and learned they had handled the same situation; so I bucked up and did it. Then I felt good about having addressed and finalized what seemed like a massive issue.

I can say from experience, you too can manage the things that overwhelm you—necessary things that have your name written on them.

If you have a home mortgage, you can skip over the following part, but if you own your home, you will find it helpful. You must set aside funds to pay the insurance and taxes. The money will not magically appear. If you have enough reserves in your checking account to cover it, fine, but some don't. Determine the yearly taxes and insurance costs, and divide it by twelve, and that is how much you need to set aside each month so that you aren't caught off guard. (Depending on how soon the next balance is due, of course.)

Consideration also might be given to whether you will have to pay income tax.

After my husband died, I got a six-month extension so that I wouldn't have to deal with income tax issues immediately. Because he died overseas and I had to ship everything back, I had no clue where the information was that I needed for taxes anyway. An extension might be of help to you if you are having trouble dealing with this issue, unless you are super organized and have everything at your fingertips.

FOURTH – LOOK AROUND YOU.

What can you live without? There are probably many things in or around your house that are just clutter that might bring some cash. Can you sell something safely online or through your local newspaper? If you work, can you post an ad on a bulletin board? How about items such as:

- A boat
- An extra car
- Antiques
- Books
- Camping gear
- Collectibles
- Fishing gear
- Furniture
- Guns
- Hunting gear
- Musical instruments
- Old electronics
- Scuba gear
- Tea sets

Could you barter for something you need? Perhaps you could trade a gun for some beef, or if you are a computer geek, help someone and in return get some work done on your car, a perm, or have a family photo taken.

Do you have marketable skills? How about starting a cottage industry?

Here are a few suggestions:

- Medical transcriptionist
- Making simple jewelry and selling it on Etsy.com
- Selling through home parties (such as cosmetics, jewelry, candles, etc.)
- Preparing documents such as work résumés
- Translating for court cases, etc.
- Teaching children who need remedial help
- Handcrafts
- Teaching English to those needing help with it as a second language
- Digitally converting photos or videos to DVDs
- Check out www.wahm.com – a resource site for work-at-home moms
- Copywriting
- Grant writing
- Publicist
- Money-making websites
- Auto responder copywriting

Fifth – Look up.

We need the Lord's help, and He has promised to establish the borders of widows.

When I returned to the Northwest and finally got my home set up about four months after Warren died, I felt a strong need to again have a regular devotion time each morning. It became my time not only to read and pray, but also my time to weep. As I knelt each morning before going to work, my routine included praying and crying until I cried it out. I didn't wail, or run around the house shouting at God and feeling sorry for myself. It was instead a pouring out of my heart in relief to the Lord who loved me, because I needed His comfort so much. He seemed near and real to me. I am sure He put His solacing arms about me and drew me close many times.

There truly is a time when the hurt is not as sharp as at first. Although our loved ones will remain in our thoughts and hearts, we are slowly able to begin a different journey without feeling that we are betraying them.

Shout It

"He will regard the prayer of the destitute, and not despise their prayer" (Ps. 102:17).

Reflect on These Questions

CHAPTER 16 QUESTIONS

Finances

1. When your husband died, by what percentage did your previous income decrease?

2. What did you have to cut back on?

3. How did you learn to be resourceful and stay within your budget (e.g. reading articles online, going to the library, talking to friends about tips on saving, couponing)?

4. How did the Lord meet your needs in very special ways?

It's True

"And it shall come to pass, that before they call, I will answer: and while they are yet speaking, I will hear" (Isa. 65:24).

Additional comprehensive questions are provided in chapter sixteen of:

A Companion Journal,
Good Grief—I Need Relief! A Widow's Guide to Recovering and Rejoicing.

Chapter Seventeen

A WIDOW'S ANSWERED PRAYERS

$\mathcal{D}$o you believe the Lord hears your prayers? Do you know that He answers them? He tells us to call on Him and He will answer. Here are two special occasions where I believe the Lord definitely answered my prayers. See if you agree.

WHERE'S THE GOOD?

(A True Story)

The night the patio wall blew down, my security system's two alert signals sent chills down my spine. I scurried to disarm it. (I had only thirty seconds before it notified the police!) My heart pounded as I glanced into the dining room, and kitchen. No sign of anyone there. Nobody in the living room, either. I rounded the corner into the laundry room to the security panel. The door beside it appeared closed.

So what on earth...?

The alarm went into emergency mode. I trembled as I tried to tune out the shrill noise and punched in the numbers. I took a deep breath in the silence that followed. I waited for my pulse to slow as I examined the door and realized it was the culprit. The suction of the heavy wind had slightly opened the door, which triggered the sensitive alarm.

Do I have to replace the door a week before Christmas? What would that do to my budget?

I walked meekly back to bed.

The Lord slept through a storm; maybe I can also. It wasn't long before I realized I was NOT the Lord, and I couldn't shut out the noise of the blustery wind outside. I tossed aside the covers and rolled out of bed again.

A quick survey through the glass sliding door revealed the gate standing open; latching it could prove more of an adventure than I cared to try.

After climbing back in bed, I reminded the Lord, "Remember, I am a widow, and you promised to protect my borders, so please do it." But the noises of things scooting across my patio startled and unnerved me. *Was someone out there? Just what was going one?* I checked again.

Every time the wind gusted, a five-foot panel rammed into the steel railing by the patio steps, then reared back when the wind paused to take a breath, and pounded it again. Romans 8:28 came to mind but didn't seem to make sense, "And we know that all things work together for good...." I prayed, "Lord, what can be good about a vinyl panel coming down and making so much noise that I can't sleep? Please show me the good."

The wind continued its pranks all night. I dozed a little, then woke up and talked to the Lord again. "Lord, did you plan all this so I could get more insurance money than I needed for repairs so I could replace the door which has set the alarm off a couple of other times? I can't wait to call the insurance company in the morning."

Moments later, the Lord impressed me that *the view will be different in the morning.* Somehow the night slowly ebbed away, but not the wind.

The starkness of the scene the next morning took away my breath. The panel, at last broken by the wind, lay on the ground. The gate, drug by the wind to the opposite side of the patio, lay smashed beyond repair. Its handle still clung to the pole which had been ripped from the gate; hinges protruded like fangs.

Just how much would all this damage cost?

I noticed that I had a few hours before I actually could call the insurance company and reach a live operator so I could file a claim. Excitedly, I looked up the number to have ready. *I wonder just how they are going to handle my situation, and how much I will have left over when the claim is paid.*

Later, I naïvely called my insurance company and explained how the wind storm (later reported to have reached 65 mph) had damaged my property. Since I didn't know the size of the panel or gate, I volunteered to measure them so she could get an estimate of the replacement cost online. The wind still blew so hard that I had to leave the phone inside the house while I stepped out.

I gave her the measurements. She countered with some bad news: I had a $1,000 deductible each time I turned in a claim. Did I think that it would cost more than that to replace the panel and the gate? I told her I didn't really know, but I doubted it. "$1,000 deductible, are you sure?" I asked. She double-checked. She was sure.

I totally rejected the idea of spending $1,000 of my emergency money with the possibility of another storm knocking the gate and fence back down. And if I chose to do it, the lady told me my insurance rates would go up on top of it! What a no-win situation.

Where's the good here, Lord? How can I get the door fixed and the mess cleaned up in the backyard?

After the wind moved away, I surveyed the damage. I didn't see any shingles lying on the ground, so I guessed the roof must be all right. I took some pictures, and then took time to make the place look normal again by up righting the planters, hanging up the bird feeder, and returning the hefty wooden bench to an upright position.

Tumbleweeds littered the back yard and presented a different problem. I didn't have room to burn them and they were too large and full of stickers to poke into a yard bag, or even try to stuff into a box and set out as garbage. Would I have to hire a teenager to come in and smash and bag them?

What was it the Lord had said last night? Ah, yes, I remembered: *the view will be different in the morning.* With the panel down, I would be able to see the small Japanese maple in the courtyard. I could see God's creation, and not just a vinyl fence. And in the spring, I could plant miniature daffodils around the base of it.

He was right. When I looked beyond the destruction, I could visualize myself resting and meditating on a stone bench, enjoying the flowers blooming around me. How charming would that be?

I couldn't wait to find some bulbs that I could start indoors and later transplant around the Japanese maple. I hoped spring came early!

The storm taught me several things:

- The Lord has a definite purpose for storms and His plan is always better than mine.

- He can provide for my needs without the insurance company. In this case, a senior saint in my church fixed my door for the price of parts.

- He gave me strength (with the help of a stepstool) to heave the tumbleweeds over the six-foot fence by the road where they came from, and a city crew later burned them.

- The Lord hears and answers prayer; and He does protect the border of widows.

Just as the Lord knocked down my physical wall, He wants to smash my walls of sin that surround me, be they bitterness, coldness of heart, greed, hatefulness, jealousy, power, pride, or anything else that fences Him out.

Yes, storms can wreck havoc, thus opening up new vistas, and bringing new possibilities. First Corinthians 13:12 says, "For now we see through a glass, darkly; but then face to face: now I know in part; but then shall I know even as also I am known."

Will I allow the Master Builder to take down my spiritual fences so that I can enjoy a renewed view of His holiness?

HELP, LORD!

(A Second True Story)

"Help, Lord! Help me!" I screamed as I hung suspended in a centrifugal force that held me in the awkward position of facing the ground as my car circled, crossed the street, and headed in the direction of my neighbor's house.

My unusual day started as I backed out of my driveway and spied a beer can lying on the edge of my lawn, carelessly tossed there during the night by some smart-alecky driver. Great witness to my lost neighbors!

I stopped, left the door open, picked up the can, walked across the driveway, and tossed it in the garbage can.

As I turned toward the car, I saw it moving backward! I sprinted across the driveway, but the car started to circle, crossed the street, and headed in the direction of my neighbor's house. Instead, it rode the curb, turned and started back toward me!

As I grabbed the door and jumped in, I realized it was going much faster than I calculated! I yanked on the door and tried to close it, but instead, the centrifugal force pulled me back toward the door and it opened wider and stretched me full length taking my face toward the pavement.

The awkward position left me suspended; my foot couldn't reach the brake. *Will I get pulled under the car?*

I tried to pull harder on the door to close it as I screamed, "Help, Lord! Help me!" I clung to the steering wheel, finally up-righting myself in the seat enough to reach and hit the brake. The car by then had completed the second circle and the back tires rested on my neighbor's sidewalk.

I trembled. *What on earth had happened? How*

could my car take off by itself? I tried to gather my thoughts as a car came up on my right side, slowed, and stopped in the street. I motioned a couple of times for them to go around me, not realizing it was my neighbor. She parked and walked over.

"Are you all right?" she asked as she glanced in and noticed my ashen face.

"I think so. Did you see what just happened?"

"No, I just pulled up."

I briefly described what occurred, and finished by saying, "I have to get to work."

"Get out, and I will pull your car into your driveway."

I willingly did so.

"You need to call work and tell them you will come in late, and go take a rest."

She handed me the keys, as I thanked her and gave her a hug.

I truly knew the truth of Psalm 124:8, "Our help is in the name of the Lord, who made heaven and earth."

When I moved into my neighborhood two years prior, I had asked the Lord to help me reach out to my neighbors. This particular neighbor hadn't responded well. So how else could God work, except through a traumatic happening, for me to hug my neighbor whose name I didn't even remember?

God orchestrated seven things in His "just right timing."

- First, the beer can was thrown in such a way that I spotted it immediately.

- Second, I left the house at the exact moment I was supposed to, which allowed the accident to occur and my neighbor to return home while I remained in the car in shock.

- Third, there were no school children on the sidewalk as they were already in school.

- Fourth, the area had no parked cars.

- Fifth, no one else came to my aid.

- Sixth, the car traveled at an angle that allowed it to miss the street sign, the neighbor's lawn, their house, and there was no damage to me or my car.

- Seventh, where the car stopped signaled the neighbor I needed help.

That day I realized God worked everything in His providence to answer my prayer of reaching out to someone in my neighborhood.

I praised the Lord it happened, and I couldn't wait to take her a thank you card and some home baked goodies.

Blessed

"And I caused the widow's heart to sing for joy"
(Job 29:13b).

I encourage you, dear widow, not to give up when you
don't have your prayers answered right away. Keep on
asking, seeking, and knocking.
He loves you and He will answer.

Reflect on These Questions

CHAPTER 17 QUESTIONS

Answered Prayers

1. What special prayers has the Lord answered for you?

2. Tell about an incident when the timing proved it was a God thing and it answered one of your prayers.

3. What lessons did you learn through your experiences?

4. How can you use these for good in the future (e.g. share with grandkids, write them up and submit them for publication, prepare them for a Bible study group with a worksheet, etc.)?

5. What storm in your life has the Lord used to teach you something special?

Blessed

"Every day will I bless thee; and I will praise thy name for
ever and ever" (Ps. 145:2).

Additional comprehensive questions are provided
in chapter seventeen of:

A Companion Journal,
Good Grief—I Need Relief! A Widow's Guide to
Recovering and Rejoicing.

Chapter Eighteen

STEPPING INTO A NEW LIFE'S PURPOSE

One day it truly sank into my soul: God was not punishing me; He actually had something He wanted me to do for Him. He left me here for a particular purpose. That realization made me look at life in a totally different way. (I don't mean this in a trite way; this truly changed my outlook on life.)

Just what was that continuing purpose? After praying and seeking the Lord's will, I found there were several:

- To help in a Children's Bible Club so I have a touch with children since my grandchildren live far away.
- To minister to other widows through visitation, luncheons, and grief classes.
- To encourage women through a devotional radio broadcast entitled *Rejoicing with Joyce.*
- To provide a home and care for my aging mother.
- To facilitate a GriefShare program.

- To remain faithful in church attendance.
- To live by faith as a witness to other widows of the grace of God in meeting my needs.
- To help support other missionaries who continue to serve in their fields.
- To be the answer to someone's prayers.

Here is an example from a text about my nine-year-old granddaughter:

> "I wish you could have seen Monique when she opened your card—arms in the air, jumping up and down, and yelling, "God answered my prayer!! God answered my prayer!!" I asked, "What were you praying for?" And she replied, "Money for my church savings!!" So, to explain, she made a commitment in October to give $1 every week above her general and missions giving for our debt retirement program. Whenever she gets extra money she sets some of it aside for that commitment, but she was about to run out of money. So she has been praying and today God answered her prayer when she got your card. :) Just thought you would enjoy knowing it."

Later, a second text read:

> "The "rest of the story" is that less than a week later our church held its annual Stewardship Banquet. Monique sat in church contemplating her commitment card and finally turned to me and said, "I really think God wants me to start giving $5 a week to

our debt retirement program instead of just $1." I about had a heart attack. I thought, "Where in the world is a nine-year-old going to find $5 a week?" But God has faithfully provided for her and she has learned so much about giving. All because you chose to obey God's prompting when he told you to send her that money...amazing what God has done in her little heart."

Consider

To behold something pleasant, refreshes our senses;
To understand a spiritual truth, refreshes our spirit;
To draw near to God, blesses our heart.

HOW CAN WE LIVE A PROFITABLE LIFE?

Here are a few ideas from other widows who chose to live profitable lives rather than assuming the fetal position:

1. One widow donated money to build a church and living quarters in a tribal village in northern Thailand for a young national pastor. (From Jan. 5, 2014 *Baptist Bread*)

2. Some widows help a women's shelter in another country, which aids abused women with alcoholic husbands. They also provide "Hear It Now MP3's" so the women can hear the salvation message.

3. Some have donated funds through their local church to help missionaries administer aid to disaster victims.

4. Bibles have been purchased for prison and jail ministries.

5. Widows have written books. (Profits from this book will go toward mission's projects.)

6. Many have volunteered at a hospital gift shop.

7. A widow who couldn't drive gave her friend some money to shop and fix a meal for a lady needing an organ donor.

8. Another widow used her art abilities to make greeting cards for the birthdays and anniversaries of our missionaries.

9. One woman donated some of her handcrafted jewelry to benefit mission's projects.

10. A widow held a yard sale and donated the money to a specific organization that helped churches build radio stations.

11. Some help with mission's conference projects at their churches.

12. Widows can coordinate the organizing of a grief support group.

13. One woman held a luncheon on her patio for other recently widowed women.

14. Another widow became a church secretary.

15. A widow took a grief seminar on "Death, Grief, & Mourning: Essential Caregiving Principles and Practices" at a funeral home to be able to reach out and companion widows better.

16. One widow speaks to ladies groups about experiencing widowhood.

Maybe you are thinking *how can I move past my hurt when my heart and my head still ache?* Here are some practical ideas and suggestions from a widow who wishes to bless you anonymously:

"If I feel I am getting depressed," she snapped her fingers and said, "I take action immediately!"

1. I call someone and chat.

2. I take a shower and get dressed up.

3. I then go out of the house and do something.

4. Or if I stay home, I clean the house, and the drawers.

5. I talk to a relative.

6. I travel and go out with friends.

Her son said, "Mom, do things that you never did before." So she did. She took piano lessons, a class on how to make crocheted purses, she learned to use the computer (she does Facebook), and she is also taking English lessons. Her daughter said, "Mom, you lost your job. You took good care of Dad for two years. That was your job, and now you have to find other things to do." She has.

More Practical Ways for Widows to Make a Difference

A new-to-me-friend, introduced by another widow, helped me in several ways:

- Although she was sick with cancer, she reached out to welcome us to the neighborhood. We decided that when things settled down, we would do early morning walks together. Her illness progressed quickly so we never realized our goal.

- She climbed on a chair and helped hang sheets over our glass sliding door so that mom and I could spend the first night in our home.

- She gave us a tour of her yard, and showed us how she planted strawberry plants among her flowers.

- She gave us flower seeds from her garden; they still live in our garden as a reminder of her friendship.

- She proved her frugality by using a homemade trellis covered with ivy to shade her patio rather than spending money on covering the whole thing.

- She gathered hurting women together once a month for lunch, and encouraged them to share prayer requests.

A Farewell Tea Party

I attended an unusual tea party, which was hosted by the out-of-town daughter of a widow with cancer. The ladies of our church were invited for tea one Saturday morning at the home of a widow under hospice care. She requested each lady bring her favorite teacup and a dozen cookies. What appropriate gift could I take? A greeting card. (She had mastered the craft of making cards and never made two alike. The recipients were always blessed.)

I began the card, "Some Golden Day Break, Jesus Will Come. Won't it be wonderful to celebrate forever around God's throne with our husbands?" Then I reminisced about special times and pleasant memories that we shared. Over forty other ladies had the privilege of reliving special moments with her as she lay in bed at her "Farewell Tea."

MORE WAYS TO FOCUS ON OTHERS

- One widow invited her neighbor to church and she got saved. Later her adult grandson followed and did the same.

- School children on the island of Fiji received Bibles distributed in their school from an offering a widow sent.

- One widow donated her husband's musical instruments to a missionary who ran an orphanage. The children enjoyed using them.

- Funds were sent to help rebuild a national pastor's house and his church after both were destroyed by a flood. Why? "...Every man according to his ability, determined to send relief unto the brethren which also they did" (Acts 11:29-30a).

- Some widows have participated in all night prayer meetings at their church.

- Online classes have been taken by some.

- One immediately continued working her bus route.

- Another widow volunteered in her church's thrift store (the profits go to world missions).

- One lady housed a foreign student so she could study at the school in her church.

- Some widows take in boarders. "For he shall deliver the needy when he crieth; the poor also, and him that hath no helper" (Ps. 72:12).

- Online grief sites have brought relief to many widows who enjoyed writing and sharing their feelings and thoughts for the day.

- A remarried widow, Ferree Hardy, writes a blog, which has encouraging, interesting information, and hundreds of faithful followers. She also seeks to provide and help start online and local widows groups using her book, *Postcards From The Widows' Path*. Here are some of Ferree's tips for new widows. [ii]

TOP TEN TIPS FOR NEW WIDOWS

If you were my sister, my mother, or a dear friend and your husband had just died, here are the ten things I'd tell you to successfully navigate the waters of widowhood:

1. **Trust God.** Easier said than done, I know. But just do it, one step, one breath at a time.

2. **Take care of your kids and/or grandkids.** They just lost their father and/or grandfather; they need you more than they can say.

3. **Get counseling.** Attend a GRIEFSHARE group (for group information in your area go to: www.griefshare.org), find a local grief or widows support group, or see a professional Christian counselor.

4. **Give this chapter of life to God.** Widowed author, Sandra Aldrich, decided to "tithe" her years of life like she tithed her financial giving. This gave her great freedom in the use of her time and in setting priorities.

5. **Rest.** It's OK to do nothing at times. Grief is physically exhausting. Lighten up and give yourself time to recover. Schedule a checkup with your doctor, allow yourself some breaks, and don't feel guilty about laughter or feeling happy again. Don't feel guilty about feeling sad, either.

6. **Give yourself something fun to look forward to.** For example, invite faraway friends to come visit, go to lunch with nearby friends. Find a walking partner, and a praying partner— perhaps someone you can call and pray over the phone with. Take a long drive if you like to drive. Sign up for a class, join the church choir...begin to re-discover interests you put away when you were married.... Finding activities I enjoyed gave me things to look forward to and helped me endure those down days when the house was one person too empty.

(To see her complete list of
Ten Top Tips for New Widows, go to:
http://www.widowschristianplace.com/2014/01/
top-tips-for-new-widows.html).

Moving On

"Thou wilt shew me the path of life: in thy presence is fullness of joy; at thy right hand there are pleasures for evermore" (Ps. 16:11).

Reflect on These Questions

CHAPTER 18 QUESTIONS

Stepping Into a New Life's Purpose

1. What special way can you welcome a newbie widow to your neighborhood?

2. How can you help a friend who recently joined the ranks of widowhood? (If she is out of your area, try a search on www.GriefShare.com to see if a group exists in her town).

3. Which idea/ideas from this chapter can you make a reality in your life?

4. What is the first step you need to take?

5. How soon can you start?

Marching Orders

"So teach us to number our days, that we may apply our hearts unto wisdom" (Ps. 90:12).

Additional comprehensive questions are provided in chapter eighteen of:

A Companion Journal,
Good Grief—I Need Relief! A Widow's Guide to Recovering and Rejoicing

Part Four

Looking Up

"For as the heavens are higher than the earth,
so are my ways higher than your ways,
and my thoughts than your thoughts" (Isaiah 55:9).

Chapter Nineteen

∾ SPIRITUAL HELPS ∾
WHO DOESN'T NEED THEM?

"*Today* (about a year and a half after my husband died, my journal read), something happened that I regretfully record. I had just read the Bible and was praying and sensing the presence of the Lord, when I suddenly popped up from my knees and began getting dressed for the day. I can't imagine why I would do such a strange thing! It is so unlike me. As soon as I had taken five or six steps, I thought *why I am I doing this?* Yet I didn't turn back and kneel."

I further noted: "I tried to finish writing a devotional today, but it didn't happen."

The day became super busy. As I finished the evening cutting back the lavender bush, I realized my goals for my devotional program had not been met. Why? Then I thought back to the beginning of the day; I didn't pause and linger. I think one of the reasons I didn't pause was anxiety seemed to shove me on, not content that I wanted to be still.

As I climbed into bed, I confessed my sin and the guilt I had carried all day. I spent a few minutes having a heart-to-heart talk with God. "Please, forgive me for starting the day in such an abrupt way. Lord, give me more love for You and others, and use me to reach people in foreign lands; even though I feel You want me to remain in Pasco."

Dear widows, even though I desired to live closer and closer to the Lord, I failed many times. Don't be too hard on yourself when you have setbacks. God loves you and me, and forgives us when we ask.

Verses that Refreshed and Replenished My Soul

Through the years as I read my Bible each day, I journaled verses which impressed me and gave me peace, so I could read them again later and receive a second blessing. I hope they will also encourage you. Pick out a category and select a verse that fits your needs, or read through them all. They will lift your spirits in trying times when you need a touch from God.

Abundant Life

"I am come that they might have life, and that they might have it more abundantly" (John 10:10).

"With God all things are possible" (Matt. 19:26).

BITTERNESS

"Let all bitterness, and wrath, and anger, and clamour, and evil speaking, be put away from you, with all malice: And be ye kind one to another, tenderhearted, forgiving one another, even as God for Christ's sake hath forgiven you" (Eph. 4:31-32).

BLESSINGS

"I will bless thee...and thou shalt be a blessing" (Gen. 12:2).

"Bless the Lord, O my soul, and forget not all His benefits" (Ps. 103:2).

BROKEN HEART

"The LORD is nigh unto them that are of a broken heart; and saveth such as be of a contrite spirit" (Ps. 34:18).

"He healeth the broken in heart, and bindeth up their wounds" (Ps. 147:3).

BURDENS

"Cast thy burden upon the LORD, and he shall sustain thee: he shall never suffer the righteous to be moved" (Ps. 55:22).

CARE

"Casting all your care upon him; for he careth for you" (1 Pet. 5:7).

COMFORT

"Blessed are they that mourn: for they shall be comforted" (Matt. 5:4).

"Let, I pray Thee, Thy merciful kindness be for my comfort" (Ps. 119:76a).

"This is my comfort in my affliction: for thy word hath quickened me" (Ps. 119:50).

"I remembered thy judgments of old, O LORD; and have comforted myself" (Ps. 119:55).

"Then they cry unto the LORD in their trouble, and he bringeth them out of their distresses. He maketh the storm a calm, so that the waves thereof are still. Then are they glad because they be quiet; so he bringeth them unto their desired haven" (Ps. 119:28-30).

"Give us help from trouble: for vain is the help of man" (Ps. 119:12).

"Unless the LORD had been my help, my soul had almost dwelt in silence. When I said, My foot slippeth; thy mercy, O LORD, held me up. In the multitude of my thoughts within me thy comforts delight my soul" (Ps. 94:17-19).

"Thou, which hast shewed me great and sore troubles, shalt quicken me again, and shalt bring me up again from the depths of the earth. Thou shalt increase my greatness, and comfort me on every side" (Ps. 71:20-21).

"Reproach hath broken my heart; and I am full of heaviness: and I looked for some to take pity, but there was none; and for comforters, but I found none" (Ps. 69:20).

"For the Lord himself shall descend from heaven with a shout, with the voice of the archangel, and with the trump of God: and the dead in Christ shall rise first: Then we which are alive and remain shall be caught up together with them in the clouds, to meet the Lord in the air: and so shall we ever be with the Lord. Wherefore comfort one another with these words" (1 Thess. 4:16-18).

COURAGE

"Be of good courage, and he shall strengthen your heart, all ye that hope in the LORD" (Ps. 31:24).

"Have not I commanded thee: Be strong and of a good courage; be not afraid, neither be thou dismayed: for the LORD thy God is with thee whithersoever thou goest" (Josh. 1:9).

CRYING

"In the day when I cried thou answeredst me, and strengthenedst me with strength in my soul" (Ps. 138:3).

"I am weary with my groaning; all the night make I my bed to swim; I water my couch with my tears. Mine eye is consumed because of grief; it waxeth old because of all mine enemies. Depart from me, all ye workers of iniquity; for the LORD hath heard the voice of my weeping" (Ps. 6:6-8).

"Blessed are ye that weep now: for ye shall laugh" (Luke 6:21b).

"Be merciful unto me, O LORD: for I cry unto thee daily" (Ps. 86:3).

"The eyes of the LORD are upon the righteous, and his ears are open unto their cry" (Ps. 34:15).

"Save me, O God; for the waters are come in unto my soul. I sink in deep mire, where there is no standing: I am come into deep waters, where the floods overflow me. I am weary of my crying: my throat is dried: mine eyes fail while I wait for my God" (Ps. 69:1-3).

DEFENSE

"My soul, wait thou only upon God; for my expectation is from him. He only is my rock and my salvation: he is my defence; I shall not be moved" (Ps. 62:5-6).

DELIVERANCE

"Many are the afflictions of the righteous: but the LORD delivereth him out of them all" (Ps. 34:19).

"The angel of the LORD encampeth round about them that fear him, and delivereth them" (Ps. 34:7).

FAITH

My prayer for you is that you "...continue in the faith grounded and settled..." (Col. 1:23).

"For we are his workmanship, created in Christ Jesus unto good works, which God hath before ordained that we should walk in them" (Eph. 2:10).

FEAR

"For God hath not given us the spirit of fear; but of power, and of love, and of a sound mind" (2 Tim. 1:7).

"I sought the LORD, and he heard me, and delivered me from all my fears" (Ps. 34:4).

"The angel of the LORD encampeth round about them that fear him, and delivereth them" (Ps. 34:7).

"I will not be afraid of ten thousands of people, that have set themselves against me round about" (Ps. 3:6).

"Be strong and of a good courage, fear not, nor be afraid of them: for the LORD thy God, he it is that doth go with thee; he will not fail thee, nor forsake thee" (Deut. 31:6).

"When thou liest down, thou shalt not be afraid: yea, thou shalt lie down, and thy sleep shall be sweet" (Prov. 3:24).

FORSAKE ME NOT

"Forsake me not, O LORD: O my God, be not far from me. Make haste to help me, O Lord my salvation: (Ps. 38:21-22).

GLADNESS

"The righteous shall be glad in the LORD, and shall trust in him; and all the upright in heart shall glory" (Ps. 64:10).

GRIEF

"For in death there is no remembrance of thee: in the grave who shall give thee thanks? I am weary with my groaning; all the night make I my bed to swim: I water my couch with my tears. Mine eye is consumed because of grief; it waxeth old because of all mine enemies" (Ps. 6:5-7).

"Have mercy upon me, O LORD, for I am in trouble: mine eye is consumed with grief, yea, my soul and my belly. For my life is spent with grief, and my years with sighing: my strength faileth because of mine iniquity, and my bones are consumed" (Ps. 31:9-10).

"I waited patiently for the LORD; and he inclined unto me, and heard my cry. He brought me up also out of a horrible pit, out of the miry clay, and set my feet upon a rock, and established my goings. And he hath put a new song in my mouth, even praise unto our God: many shall see it, and fear, and shall trust in the LORD" (Ps. 40:1-3).

GUIDANCE

"The Lord shall guide thee continually and satisfy thy soul..." (Isa. 58:11a).

"Cause me to hear thy lovingkindness in the morning; for in thee do I trust: cause me to know the way wherein I should walk; for I lift up my soul unto thee" (Ps. 143:8).

HEALTH

"Why art thou cast down, O my soul? And why art thou disquieted within me? Hope in God: for I shall yet praise him, who is the health of my countenance, and my God" (Ps. 43:5).

HELP

"Be not dismayed; for I am thy God: I will strengthen thee; yea, I will help thee..." (Isa. 41:10b).

"Because thou hast been my help, therefore in the shadow of thy wings will I rejoice" (Ps. 63:7).

"Hear me speedily, O Lᴏʀᴅ: my spirit faileth: hide not thy face from me, lest I be like unto them that go down into the pit" (Ps. 143:7).

"Our help is in the name of the Lᴏʀᴅ, who made heaven and earth" (Ps. 124:8).

HOPE

"Now the God of hope fill you with all joy and peace in believing, that ye may abound in hope, through the power of the Holy Ghost" (Rom. 15:13).

"Be of good courage, and he shall strengthen your heart, all ye that hope in the Lᴏʀᴅ" (Ps. 31:24).

"For in thee, O Lᴏʀᴅ, do I hope: thou wilt hear, O Lord my God" (Ps. 38:15).

"Why art thou cast down, O my soul? And why art thou disquieted in me? Hope thou in God; for I shall yet praise him for the help of his countenance" (Ps. 42:5).

JOY

"...And their soul shall be as a watered garden; and they shall not sorrow any more at all...for I will turn their mourning into joy, and will comfort them, and make them rejoice from their sorrow" (Jer. 31:12-13).

"Thou wilt shew me the path of life: in thy presence is fullness of joy; at thy right hand there are pleasures for evermore" (Ps. 16:11).

"For ye shall go out with joy, and be led forth with peace..." (Isa. 55:12a)

LEAD ME

"For thou art my rock and my fortress; therefore for thy name's sake lead me, and guide me" (Ps. 31:3).

LIFE'S PURPOSE

"...Take heed to the ministry which thou hast received in the Lord, that thou fulfil it" (Col. 4:17).

"I waited patiently for the LORD: and he inclined unto me, and heard my cry. He brought me up also out of an horrible pit, out of the miry clay, and set my foot upon a rock, and established my goings. And he hath put a new song in my mouth, even praise unto our God: many shall see it, and fear, and shall trust in the LORD" (Ps. 40:1-4).

LOVE

"Many waters cannot quench love, neither can the floods down it: if a man would give all the substance of his house for love, it would utterly be contemned" (Song of Sol. 8:7a).

"Let all those that seek thee rejoice and be glad in thee: let such as love thy salvation say continually, The LORD be magnified" (Ps. 40:16).

"For I am persuaded, that neither death, nor life, nor angels, nor principalities, nor powers, nor things present, nor things to come, nor height, nor depth, nor any other creature, shall be able to separate us from the love of God, which is in Christ Jesus our Lord" (Rom. 8:38-39).

"I love the Lord, because he hath heard my voice and my supplications. Because he hath inclined his ear unto me, therefore will I call upon him as long as I live" (Ps. 116:1-2).

"And I will delight myself in thy commandments, which I have loved" (Ps. 119:47).

"Great peace have they which love thy law: and nothing shall offend them" (Ps. 119:165).

MERCY

"Let thy mercy, O LORD, be upon us, according as we hope in thee" (Ps. 33:22).

"When I said, My foot slippeth; thy mercy, O LORD, held me up" (Ps. 94:18).

MOURNING

"Like a crane *or* a swallow, so did I chatter: I did mourn as a dove: mine eyes fail *with looking* upward: O LORD, I am oppressed; undertake for me." (Isa. 38:14).

OUR WAYS

"But none of these things move me, neither count I my life dear unto myself, so that I might finish my course with joy, and the ministry which I have received of the Lord Jesus, to testify the gospel of the grace of God" (Acts 20:24).

"I have fought a good fight, I have finished my course, I have kept the faith: Henceforth there is laid up for me a crown of righteousness, which the Lord, the righteous judge, shall give me at that day: and not to me only, but unto all them also that love his appearing" (2 Tim. 4:6-8).

"For our light affliction, which is but for a moment, worketh for us a far more exceeding and eternal weight of glory; While we look not at the things which are seen, but at the things which are not seen: for the things which are seen are temporal; but the things which are not seen are eternal" (2 Cor. 4:17-18).

"Cause me to hear thy lovingkindness in the morning; for in thee do I trust: cause me to know the way wherein I should walk; for I lift up my soul unto thee" (Ps. 143:8).

OVERWHELMED

"When my spirit was overwhelmed within me, then thou knewest my path" (Ps. 142:3a).

PEACE

"...Live in peace; and the God of love and peace shall be with you" (2 Cor. 13:11b).

"In Him we live, and move, and have our being" (Acts 17:28).

"Thou wilt keep him in perfect peace, whose mind is stayed on Thee" (Isa. 26:3).

"Hear my prayer, O LORD, and give ear unto my cry; hold not thy peace at my tears..." (Ps. 39:12a).

PRAISE AND THANKSGIVING

"From the rising of the sun unto the going down of the same the Lord's name is to be praised" (Ps. 113:3).

"The LORD is righteous in all his ways, and holy in all his works" (Ps. 145:17).

"It is a good thing to give thanks unto the LORD, and to sing praises unto thy name, O most High: To shew forth thy lovingkindness in the morning, and thy faithfulness every night" (Ps. 92:1-2).

"O LORD, thou art my God; I will exalt thee, I will praise thy name; for thou hast done wonderful things; thy counsels of old are faithfulness and truth. For thou hast been a strength to the poor, a strength to the needy in his distress, a refuge from the storm, a shadow from the heat, when the blast of the terrible ones is as a storm against the wall" (Isa. 25:1, 4).

PRAYER

"And all things, whatsoever ye shall ask in prayer, believing, ye shall receive" (Matt. 21:22).

"He will regard the prayer of the destitute, and not despise their prayer" (Ps. 102:17).

"My voice shalt thou hear in the morning, O LORD; in the morning will I direct my prayer unto thee, and will look up" (Ps. 5:3).

"Again I say unto you, That if two of you shall agree on earth as touching any thing that they shall ask, it shall be done for them of my Father which is in heaven. For where two or three are gathered together in my name, there am I in the midst of them" (Matt. 18:19-20).

POSSIBILITIES

"But Jesus beheld them, and said unto them, With men this is impossible; but with God all things are possible" (Matt. 19:26).

REFUGE

"Trust in him at all times; ye people, pour out your heart before him: God is a refuge for us. Selah" (Ps. 62:8).

"The eternal God is thy refuge, and underneath are the everlasting arms" (Deut. 33:27a).

"The LORD also will be a refuge for the oppressed, a refuge in times of trouble. And they that know thy name will put their trust in thee: for thou, LORD, hast not forsaken them that seek thee" (Ps. 9:9-10).

REJOICE

"Thou has made known to me the ways of life; thou shalt make me full of joy with thy countenance" (Acts 2:28).

"O satisfy us early with Thy mercy; that we may rejoice and be glad all our days" (Ps. 90:14).

"But let all those that put their trust in thee rejoice: let them ever shout for joy, because thou defendest them: let them also that love thy name be joyful in thee" (Ps. 5:11).

"I will be glad and rejoice in thee: I will sing praise to thy name, O thou most High" (Ps. 9:2).

SLEEP

"It is vain for you to rise up early, to sit up late, to eat the bread of sorrows: for so he giveth his beloved sleep" (Ps. 127:2).

"I will both lay me down in peace, and sleep: for thou, LORD, only makest me dwell in safety" (Ps. 4:8).

"I laid me down and slept; I awaked; for the LORD sustained me" (Ps. 3:5).

SORROW

"A merry heart maketh a cheerful countenance: but by sorrow of the heart the spirit is broken" (Prov. 15:13).

STRENGTH

"In quietness and in confidence shall be your strength" (Isa. 30:15).

"He giveth power to the faint; and to them that have no might he increaseth strength. Even the youths shall faint and be weary, and the young men shall utterly fall: But they that wait upon the LORD shall renew their strength; they shall mount up with wings as eagles; they shall run, and not be weary; and they shall walk, and not faint" (Isa. 40:29-31).

TEACH AND LEAD ME

"Teach me to do thy will; for thou art my God: thy spirit is good; lead me into the land of uprightness" (Ps. 143:10).

"Lead me, O LORD, in thy righteousness because of mine enemies; make thy way straight before my face" (Ps. 5:8).

"Thou wilt shew me the path of life: in thy presence is fullness of joy; at thy right hand there are pleasures for evermore" (Ps. 16:11).

TEARS

"Hear my prayer, O LORD, and give ear unto my cry; hold not thy peace at my tears..." (Ps. 39:12).

TROUBLE

"God is our refuge and strength, a very present help in trouble. Therefore will not we fear, though the earth be removed, and though the mountains be carried into the midst of the sea; Though the waters thereof roar and be troubled, though the mountains shake with the swelling thereof. Selah" (Ps. 46:1-3).

"But I will sing of thy power; yea, I will sing aloud of thy mercy in the morning: for thou hast been my defence and refuge in the day of my trouble" (Ps. 59:16).

"This poor man cried, and the LORD heard him, and saved him out of all his troubles" (Ps. 34:6).

TRUST

"Trust in the LORD with all thine heart; and lean not unto thine own understanding. In all thy ways acknowledge him, and he shall direct thy paths" (Prov. 3:5-6).

"Trust in him at all times; ye people, pour out your heart before him: God is a refuge for us. Selah" (Ps. 62:8).

"The righteous shall be glad in the LORD, and shall trust in him; and all the upright in heart shall glory" (Ps. 64:10).

VOWS

"...I will pay thee my vows, Which my lips have uttered, and my mouth hath spoken, when I was in trouble" (Ps. 66:13b-14).

WEAKNESS

"Have mercy upon me, O LORD; for I am weak: O LORD, heal me; for my bones are vexed. My soul is also sore vexed: but thou, O LORD, how long? Return, O LORD, deliver my soul: oh save me for thy mercies' sake" (Ps. 6:2-4).

"My soul melteth for heaviness: strengthen thou me according unto thy word" (Ps. 119:28).

WIDOW

"For he shall deliver the needy when he crieth; the poor also, and him that hath no helper" (Ps. 72:12).

"The times of refreshing shall come from the presence of the Lord" (Acts 3:19b).

"And that ye study to be quiet, and to do your own business, and to work with your own hands..." (1 Thess. 4:11).

WISDOM

"If any of you lack wisdom, let him ask of God, that giveth to all men liberally, and upbraideth not; and it shall be given him" (James 1:5).

"Happy is the man that findeth wisdom, and the man that getteth understanding" (Prov. 3:13).

"Get wisdom, get understanding: forget it not; neither decline from the words of my mouth. Forsake her not, and she shall preserve thee: love her, and she shall keep thee. Wisdom is the principal thing; therefore get wisdom: and with all thy getting get understanding. Exalt her, and she shall promote thee: she shall bring thee to honour, when thou dost embrace her" (Prov. 4:5-8).

"So teach us to number our days, that we may apply our hearts unto wisdom" (Ps. 90:12).

STOP AND ANALYZE:

"The Bible is the lamp that lights the sinner's way to Calvary. The Bible is the shawl that warms the heart of the coldest Christian. The Bible is the comforter that caresses the bereaved in the hour of deep sorrow. The Bible is the plow that breaks up the fallow ground of the backslidden.

"The Bible is the microscope that probes the depths of the soul and reveals the real you. Sick of it? No! It is the balm that heals the sin sick heart." —Tim Green [iii]

Prayer of Comfort

Lord, bless all of the widows who are still floundering in life. Hug us, love us, and direct us.

Reflect on These Questions

CHAPTER 19 QUESTIONS

Spiritual Helps

1. Record here your thoughts regarding your walk with the Lord (e.g. sporadic, faithful, dynamic, cold, etc.):

2. What progress do you plan to see soon? (e.g. I plan to study the book of_____, memorize some verses, pick a subject such as "widow" and learn as much as I can, etc.)

3. What deep hunger are you waiting for the Lord to fill in your life?

4. Have you ever been sidetracked from His presence and His Word? If so, recall how you felt and reacted.

5. What verses encouraged or blessed you?

Be Assured

"I waited patiently for the LORD; and he inclined unto me, and heard my cry. He brought me up also out of an horrible pit, out of the miry clay, and set my feet upon a rock, and established my goings. And he hath put a new song in my mouth, even praise unto our God: many shall see it, and fear, and shall trust in the LORD" (Ps. 40:1-3).

Additional comprehensive questions are provided in chapter nineteen of:

A Companion Journal,
Good Grief—I Need Relief! A Widow's Guide to Recovering and Rejoicing.

Chapter Twenty

SPIRITUAL WARFARE

No marriage is perfect, although some appear to come close to it. However, when we are at our lowest and feeling the pain of the loss of a dear one, Satan takes advantage of our weaknesses. He throws innuendos as darts of uncertainty, suspicions, and even hatred. He provokes us with insinuations and whisperings that can haunt.

Just what do I mean by that?

Perhaps your husband left his financial affairs in a mess and you feel stranded, let down and helpless. Why wasn't he more responsible? I am sure you could rant for hours but in the end you still have the same issues staring you in the face. What will you need to do to adjust and cope with the situation to be able to move forward with life? There is an answer. Search for the One who holds the key to unlock the mystery to help you. (Ask, seek, and knock.)

Or maybe your husband took his life and you feel cheated because your marriage ended on a sour note, and

232 — Good Grief—I Need Relief!

much too early for you. Perhaps you knew nothing of his troubled spirit and think if only he had been willing to talk to you more, sought counsel, just taken his medication, or whatever your particular situation might have been, he might still be alive. Stop beating yourself up because he had difficulty dealing with issues that were beyond your expertise, or over which you might have had no control even if you had known, or for which you couldn't find the right solution.

Once in a while I meet a woman who is sure she overmedicated her husband and killed him as a result. This is seldom true, but Satan enjoys playing the "what if" game.

Some widows have been left in a precarious position with doubts about their final relationship with their late husband. They feel hopeless or betrayed. Did he love me? Was he having an affair?

You may feel some of these issues cannot be resolved and have no possible future closure. If that is your case, please read on.

I was surprised to learn at a special Spiritual Warfare meeting called "Closing the Door" by Pastor Marvin E. Smith, (www.hbcfd.com) that bitterness bound me in chains that could only be removed through forgiveness. This bitterness started immediately after I returned to Japan to pack up my things. My plans didn't go like I thought they should, and at times I felt frustrated, misunderstood, and even taken advantage of, not realizing I was in the throes of grief and not thinking sanely.

However, during that meeting, I got it! I understood what had been happening to me for the past few years. The issues I just mentioned kept playing over and over in my mind and I had some deep emotions that needed to be cleared and cleaned up toward more than one person.

The Lord touched my heart with conviction over the hostility I harbored there. I went forward at the end of the meeting, dropped to my knees and prayed, "Please forgive my bitterness and close this door in my life." I named particular instances and people and He gave me immediate deliverance. He closed the door to that area in my life, gave me peace, and liberated me from dreary land. I seldom visit those memories now because the Lord removed the bitter sting from my heart and gave me freedom.

I should have realized the happiness robber was Satan. Why had I given him license to play with my mind? Ephesians 4:26-27 can be so liberating: "Be ye angry, and sin not: let not the sun go down upon your wrath: Neither give place to the devil."

Perhaps bitterness is an issue in your life, and you, like I, had no awareness that it even existed. I encourage you to let the Holy Spirit search your soul and reveal to you what stands between you and the blessings the Lord is waiting to pour out on your life. Won't you pray right now, then acknowledge it, and forsake it? Your blessing is peeking around the corner. Grab it today!

CLOSURE

"And grieve not the holy Spirit of God, whereby ye are sealed unto the day of redemption. Let all bitterness, and wrath, and anger, and clamour, and evil speaking, be put away from you, with all malice: And be ye kind one to another, tenderhearted, forgiving one another, even as God for Christ's sake hath forgiven you" (Eph. 4:30-32).

LEGACY

Satan has an aggressive agenda. Just what is it? He intends to dumb-down the importance of magnifying the Lord in our life—especially as a widow, and especially as church time approaches each week. Have you found that's when you suddenly feel sick or realize there are some chores, errands, or phone calls you simply must get done? After all, you do work (or not) and this is your only time to get these things taken care of, right? Wrong! These thoughts do not come from the Lord. He would never go against His Word, which tells us not to forsake the gathering of ourselves together (Heb. 10:25).

DISORGANIZED?

Satan delights in this one. He wants us to run late (again?) and to decide it's easier to give up and listen to, or watch, the service at home, rather than to make the effort to attend. After all, who wants the embarrassment of being late?

No Clothing?

Not sure what to wear? How about saving time by choosing what clothes you will wear the night before, and make sure they are ready to go? An excuse often used is, "I don't have anything to wear." Then shop and take care of it! A few basic pieces will take you far.

Traveling?

When Warren and I traveled, we always tried to plan where we stopped on Saturday night, so we could fellowship in a church of like faith the next day. If we weren't familiar with the area, we checked a directory to find one. Waiting to the last minute can be frustrating since sometimes directions are not the easiest to follow, although electronics have done wonders to eliminate some guesswork in this area.

Why is all of this important to us as widows?

Because we send subtle signals to our loved ones. Whether those signals are silent or otherwise, we are being read. People are watching to see where Christ ranks in our level of importance, and how high we lift His name and reverence His holiness. Do we use His name lightly or as a curse word?

COMPANY?

Whether I am a visitor, or have someone in my home, I have a predetermined plan of action. It's the answer to a situation that can be awkward. My visitors are always invited to attend church with me. If I am a guest somewhere, I usually attend with them unless it would cause me to grieve the Holy Spirit (Eph. 4:30), and make me feel uncomfortable.

GRANDMA TIME

As a mother and a grandma, how do our children and grandchildren view us? Are we lifting up the banner of faith, or letting it droop? Do we need to fly the flag higher?

For instance, when we have the opportunity, do we read or tell Bible stories to them, or play act the stories together?

What a privilege it is to be able to take a grandchild to church with you if their parents choose to stay home. I clap for you! My grandchildren live in other states, so I don't have that privilege. I love it when my children visit and I get to sit with them and my grandkids in church. I feel so blessed.

May our children say to their children, "Grandma loved the Lord, and even after Grandpa died, she attended church faithfully—as long as her health allowed."

SUBTLE SIGNALS

What subtle signals are we sending? Are they positive or negative?

- Are there scriptures on my walls?
- Do we listen to a Christian radio station or have rock music blaring in our house or car? (This can be a good testimony when we have the oil changed in our car. Leave your favorite Christian station or CD on so when they start the car, the music comes on.)
- Do we sing spiritual songs? When your family gathers, do you enjoy a "singspiration" time with familiar hymns?
- How about a Christian calendar on my wall?

These things speak volumes without uttering a word.

Ephesians 6:12 says, "For we wrestle not against flesh and blood, but against principalities, against powers, against the rulers of the darkness of this world, against spiritual wickedness in high places."

FINISH STRONG

"Wouldn't it be awful to live all your life for the Lord, and mess up at the end? I would hate that," a widowed friend said to me.

I was taken aback by her statement and stammered, "Why, yes, it would." Since I had never given much thought to it until this strong woman, who had counseled me in the past, said it, I wondered just what motivated her to even think it.

Perhaps she realized the reality of sin, the possibility that lies within us to become the next victim and a statistic. Was she warning me? Maybe, and it gave me food for thought that I want to share with you.

As widows, perhaps we are a bit naïve. We may find it hard to believe Satan wants to trip us up, but he does. He is no dummy, and he wears many disguises. Perhaps he dresses up as a gentleman in our church, a builder, repairman, poet, songwriter, neighbor, someone online, or from a dating service.

Loneliness can do strange things to people; it makes them receptors of false attention. (Meaning the attention they receive might not have good motivation behind it.)

Case in point, who was deceived in the Garden of Eden, Adam or Eve? Yes, it was the woman, wasn't it? We are such trusting creatures that our discernment is sometimes blinded to truth.

Is there anything wrong with widows watching sensuous TV programs, reading enticing books or magazines that shout, "Buy me! You know you want to!"? After all, no one is around and the story line is exciting and we want to know how it ends. Right? Score one for Satan if we fall for his deception. The more programs and books that fill our minds with lustful thoughts, the further we drift from the Lord and purity. Then it makes it easier for Satan to shoot fiery darts at us and wound us.

Guard the door to your heart, and your home!

We are instructed in 1 Peter 5:8 to, "Be sober, be vigilant; because your adversary the devil, as a roaring lion, walketh about seeking whom he may devour."

We are told to be calm and watchful so we aren't deceived by Satan who wants to totally destroy us and our testimony.

Every day I pray what people call the prayer of Jabez. It's found in 1 Chronicles 4:10: "And Jabez called on the God of Israel, saying, Oh that thou wouldest bless me indeed, and enlarge my coast, and that thine hand might be with me, and that thou wouldest keep me from evil, that it may not grieve me! And God granted him that which he requested."

I find it interesting that Jabez realized that dabbling with evil brings a penalty; it produces grief. Yes, we are troubled when we go against God's laws. It's as if we shake our fist in His face and say, "I can do what I want; I have my rights." Our rights stop where the law begins. It overrides us. We can say we have a right to go through a red light if we want too. But the law says we have to stop. If we decide to go through the light anyway, and hit someone then we must pay the penalty for our wrongdoing. The same principle applies to spiritual laws.

God says don't. We say do. Then when a consequence rears its ugly head, we back up and cry foul!

What should we do when we are tempted to commit an immoral act? Run, like Joseph did when tempted by his master's wife. Get away from the situation and determine never to be caught in that kind of a circumstance again. There is an answer; there is an escape.

First Corinthians 10:13 says, "There hath no temptation taken you but such as is common to man: but God is faithful, who will not suffer you to be tempted above that ye are able; but will with the temptation also make a way to escape, that ye may be able to bear it."

I don't want to tempt a man to sin, and neither do I want to be deceived by one. Dear widowed friend, I want the same thing for you.

Let's *finish strong* together!

Help Us Lord to Stop and Think

"For innumerable evils have compassed me about... Be pleased, O LORD, to deliver me: O LORD, make haste to help me. Let them be ashamed and confounded together that seek after my soul to destroy it; let them be driven backward and put to shame that wish me evil" (Ps. 40:12-14).

$\mathscr{R}$eflect on $\mathcal{T}$hese $\mathcal{Q}$uestions

CHAPTER 20 QUESTIONS

Spiritual Warfare

Dear widow, what situation in your life is binding you? Might it be bitterness, hatred, or denial? Whatever it is, I give you permission to free yourself by confessing and forsaking whatever issue is holding you back. It's also what the Lord wants.

1. Who or what stands between you and peace? Liberating that circumstance or person through forgiveness will liberate you.

2. Since sharing some personal information might not be what you want to leave in a legacy, why don't you take a separate piece of paper and write out the situation/situations that you want closure on, and when you have finished, pray through your list or situation. Ask the Lord to terminate the snare that Satan, the king of terrors, has laid for you. Claim the blood of Christ to free you.

God bless you as you take this important step in your life that will allow you to breathe more easily, sleep better, and take the next step in your new life—freedom.

3. Have you had a harder time getting to church since you've been widowed? What steps can you take to overcome it?

4. What good subtle signals are you giving out?

5. What organizational steps have you begun to hold your flag higher? (Refer to **"Grandma Time"**, p. 236 and **"Subtle Signals"**, p. 237 if you are stuck).

Carry His Torch

"Cause me to hear thy lovingkindness in the morning; for in thee do I trust: cause me to know the way wherein I should walk; for I lift up my soul unto thee" (Ps. 143:8).

Additional comprehensive questions are provided
in chapter twenty of:

A Companion Journal,
Good Grief—I Need Relief! A Widow's Guide to
Recovering and Rejoicing.

Chapter Twenty-One

IS THERE LIFE AFTER DEATH?

By Missionary Paul Williams

*N*o! Webster's 1828 American Dictionary defines life as, "The present state of existence; the time from birth to death," thereby defining that there is no life after death.

Really? Is that what you believe?

The age-long answer to life after death has been sought by many across time. There is an answer that is correct and truthful. Those that would dispute it simply ignore the truth that we are here for a purpose and that purpose does not end with death but continues on in what is often termed as "the afterlife."

Before you start forming an opinion about what I am saying, let me explain the answer that I gave at the beginning ("NO!"). There is something after death. For some it is eternal life but for others it is an eternal existence in a place not meant for humanity, yet our own actions place us there.

Because of the actions of Adam, the Bible tells us that we are all born into sin. Not one of us is born with an ounce of goodness. King David of Israel in Psalm 51 states, "Behold, I was shapen in iniquity; and in sin did my mother conceive me." Let me make a point. I have to admit that babies are cute and cuddly and it is difficult to think of them as being sinners. That is, until they wake you up in the middle of the night with a blood-curdling scream and on the way to their crib side you stub your toe causing you to fall headlong into the hallway nearly giving yourself a concussion as you hit the wall. All of this to find out that they just wanted to be held. There was no emergency, no snakes, no monsters, not even a wet diaper, just a selfish little sinner who wanted some attention and woke you out of a dead sleep to let you know it. And yes, you and I did that as "innocent" little babies.

When God created Adam and Eve, the misconception is that He created them as perfect and sinless beings. God created them in a state of innocence with a free will to choose between either obedience to God with eternal life or disobedience which ends in disciplinary action and eventual death. Not just death in a physical manner but everlasting death in a place created for the devil and his angels, a place called hell.

In the beginning, God created innocent humans with a will to make choices. That choice was made when Adam and Eve chose to go against God's command to not eat of the tree of knowledge of good and evil. Yet God knew what they would do before He created them. If you have children, you knew before you conceived them that they would grow up, you would have to discipline them, they might break your heart, and they might do something that would be nearly impossible to forgive. But you went ahead and had children, knowing full well what they might do yet hoping for the best.

God's plan was to create the human race so that He could have someone to prove His love to. His plan was to create us, allow us to choose the wrong direction, and then to show His merciful and unconditional love by making the decision to put our need for a Saviour before His own needs. It was this great act of love which resulted in a great sacrifice that moved God's heart to bring us back into a personal relationship with Him.

I have a wonderful relationship with each of my children and I love them equally and unconditionally. Does that mean that I always like what they do? Of course it doesn't, but they are still my children. I would do whatever I could to let them know how much I love them and that the fellowship which was broken by their acts of disobedience had caused a rift between us that I wanted to be restored. I can make the sacrifice and the effort to offer a peace offering to my children. Yet it is their choice. They can either accept the peace offering and ask for forgiveness so the relationship can be restored or reject it and continue on their own path, which would widen the rift between us.

The same situation applies to each of us. We were created by God for a purpose and we broke the fellowship with Him. We walked away. The fellowship and the relationship between us were broken and a great rift was made. In order to show His love to us, God made a peace offering through His Son, Jesus Christ. The perfect, sinless, only begotten Son of God took the punishment for our disobedience upon Himself when He came as God in the flesh, lived among us without sin, and then God laid our sin upon Him on the cross, and He died in our place. After three days in a tomb, He rose from the dead, proving that He was God and that He had the power to give life. Eternal life. The Bible states that if we confess our disobedience and sinfulness and accept the gift of God's peace offering (the payment for our sin in Christ's sacrificial death on the cross), the relationship between God and us will be restored. Then, in addition to His forgiveness and restoration of the relationship, God grants to each of us eternal life. Not eternal physical life but eternal spiritual life in Heaven with Him for all eternity.

The other choice—just like a child deciding to go his own way—is to continue on a path to eternal destruction. If we reject the peace offering and the opportunity of forgiveness, then when this physical life is over we will spend an eternity separated from God. This is a choice that each of us must make. By birth, we are born into sin and separated from God. We must choose whether or not we want to spend an eternity with Him and all of His glory and majesty, or eternity in torment, separated from God.

Yes! There is life after death. There is eternal life for those who choose it. For those who reject it, there is only eternal death. Just as I would want each of my children to choose to restore the relationship that was broken between us, so God wants each of us to choose an eternity with Him.

When a loved one dies physically and passes into eternity, we grieve. We miss them because there is an empty place in our lives. The relationship and time spent together has passed and all that remains are memories. The one hope that we have of being able to see them again is for each of us to choose forgiveness from God and to accept the gift of salvation and eternal life through Jesus Christ.

Count on It

"The LORD is nigh unto all them that call upon him, to all that call upon him in truth" (Ps. 145:18).

Reflect on These Questions

CHAPTER 21 QUESTIONS

Is There Life After Death?

1. Do you agree with Webster's 1828 American Dictionary that life ceases when we die?

   Why or why not?

2. When our children cause a rift between us and we do our best to offer a peaceable solution, they can either accept the peace offering and ask for forgiveness so the relationship can be restored, or reject it and continue on their own path which would widen the rift. Have you applied that to your own situation with the Lord?

3. Have you asked the Lord to forgive your sins and trust Him by faith to give you eternal life? If so, what was the date?_____What were the circumstances, and where did this take place? (Record it so that your family can share in the details of this life changing action.)

4. Did you follow your conversion by being baptized? If yes, where and when?

5. How did your decision change your life (e.g. I wanted to read the Bible more, I was convicted of _____in my life and prayed to have it eradicated from my life)?

God's Wish

"That all the people of the earth might know the hand of the LORD, that it is mighty: that ye might fear the LORD your God for ever" (Josh. 4:24).

Additional comprehensive questions are provided in chapter twenty-one of:

A Companion Journal,
Good Grief—I Need Relief! A Widow's Guide to Recovering and Rejoicing.

.

Chapter Twenty-Two

∽ THE FUTURE ∽
WHERE ARE MY SUNGLASSES?

It has been said that, "The future is as bright as the promises of God." However, some things might need to change before the future looks bright to you.

Lynn Brookside states it well in her meditation, *Letting Go*:

> Most of us have known or heard about people who seem to place their households in suspended animation after the death of someone close. They leave their loved one's room untouched, bed made up and ready for their return. The loved one's books and papers are set out on the desk as if they had just stepped away momentarily. It is almost as if those mourners are waiting for God to come to his senses and return their loved one to them.
>
> These grief-stricken people who simply cannot let go, seem to feel as if accepting their loss is like abandoning their loved one. It seems to them that

acceptance implies approval, even gladness, regarding their loved one's death. They don't realize that they will continue to be victimized by their loss until they've come to accept it.

You may not be living in the past, spending your time existing in your memories, but most of us experience a reluctance to let go. We need to assess, realistically, the consequences of our reluctance. The past is static. It does not adapt to our present needs. Our memory of those pleasant times when our loved one brought us joy will not nurture us or meet our needs in the present. Furthermore, we will become increasingly isolated if we continue to exist in the past while those around us are moving on with their lives.

When we refuse to let go of the past we are, in essence, saying to God, "Your timing is wrong and I don't accept it. I have a better plan and I'm not going to let you get away with this. It hurts too much and I don't trust you to walk me through this pain."

Job had a similar complaint. Job questioned God's judgment, accusing God of committing an injustice by allowing Job to be afflicted when he had done nothing wrong. God responded to Job's complaints saying, "Where were you when I laid the earth's foundation?... Who marked off its dimensions?... Have you ever given orders to the morning, or shown the dawn its place?" Job was forced to reply, "Surely I spoke of things I did not understand, things too wonderful for me to know" (see Job 38-42).

It's the same for us. When we rage against our loss we are questioning God's judgment. We speak of things we do not understand. Naturally we are angry because death overtakes us like a storm, usually without warning. We are helpless to stop it. But we will continue to feel victimized by it until we let go. Letting go doesn't mean forgetting our loved one or being glad for his or her death. It does mean accepting God's will for our lives and bowing to his sovereignty.

If you feel that you are ready to say a final good-bye to your loved one, today would be a good day to plan a farewell ritual. Write your loved one a letter. Express how much you miss him or her. Describe your sorrow over the death of your dreams for the shared future you will never have. Then sign the letter and say good-bye.[iv]

Press on with anticipation.

Just what does the future hold for me? Only the Lord knows. However, I am assured that whatever it is, "He works all things for (our) good" (Rom. 8:28).

What gets you out of bed with a bound, making you look forward to what the Lord has placed in your heart to accomplish for the day? I find Bible study is exciting once again, and I enjoy spending time in God's Word. If you don't, why not ask the Lord to give you a subject to research and take notes on what you learn? Then you will have something to share when someone asks you to speak, or when you have a chance to explain to a family member what blessings you've received recently. You might be pleasantly surprised to learn that you actually do enjoy your time with the Lord each day.

My devotional time spent on my back patio porch swing in the morning refreshes me as my eyes focus on the deep green of the ferns, the pink and rose of the dogwood tree, the lavender flowers on the moss, the yellow and burgundy chrysanthemums, all set to the hedge of the arborvitae trees which have topped the fence since they were planted. As I sit and drink in the beauty of God's creation, my mind wanders and I wonder what the Garden of Eden looked like. One day I hope the Lord allows us to see it.

What does my future hold? It's a mystery known only to God, but I am anticipating an exciting journey.

Here are some of Oswald Chambers' thoughts on it:

WHAT'S NEXT TO DO?

"The counterfeit of obedience is a state of mind in which you create your own opportunities to sacrifice yourself, and your zeal and enthusiasm are mistaken for discernment. It is easier to sacrifice yourself than to fulfill your spiritual destiny, which is stated in Romans 12:1-2. It is much better to fulfill the purpose of God in your life by discerning His will than it is to perform great acts of self-sacrifice. 'Behold, to obey is better than sacrifice...' (1 Samuel 15:22). Beware of paying attention or going back to what you once were, when God wants you to be something that you have never been. 'If anyone wills to do His will, he shall know...' (John 7:17)."ᵛ

Cherish

"Hear, O Lᴏʀᴅ, and have mercy upon me: Lord, be thou my helper. Thou hast turned for me my mourning into dancing: thou hast put off my sackcloth, and girded me with gladness; To the end that my glory may sing praise to thee, and not be silent. O Lᴏʀᴅ my God, I will give thanks unto thee for ever" (Ps. 30:10-12).

Reflect on These Questions

CHAPTER 22 QUESTIONS

The Future

Being a widow can be exciting as well as exhausting. I pray your days are becoming easier and you can see through the fog that once clouded your horizon. Although the hurt in your heart is always there, it does dim with time. If you aren't there yet, just know that happier days lie ahead, and they will come. Isn't that good news?

1. In a couple of sentences, write out the vision the Lord has placed on your heart for the horizon of your tomorrows. I pray that you execute His plan and purpose for your life. (Perhaps a new business? Building a house? Traveling? Retraining? Writing?)

2. Just what project makes you want to jump out of bed and get started (working in your yard, writing, helping a neighbor, getting your new business set up, etc.)?

3. What favorite spot calls to you when it's time for your devotions?

4. What dream have you not given up on?
   Name it and do it!

5. How can you help yourself move forward?

Enjoy These

"Teach me to do thy will; for thou art my God: thy spirit is good; lead me into the land of uprightness" (Ps. 143:10).

"Cause me to hear thy lovingkindness in the morning; for in thee do I trust: cause me to know the way wherein I should walk; for I lift up my soul unto thee" (Ps. 143:8).

Additional comprehensive questions are provided
in chapter twenty-two of:

*A Companion Journal,
Good Grief—I Need Relief! A Widow's Guide to
Recovering and Rejoicing.*

Chapter Twenty-Three

∽ LEGACY ∽
THE REST OF THE STORY

$\mathcal{O}$ne day Lt. Commander Dan Todd said to my husband, "I think you need to create little Warren Webster's who will become future preachers like you." The idea germinated and my husband started a Preacher Boys class on Saturday nights after the regularly scheduled prayer time.

Although the church already held a video Bible Institute which provided basic knowledge of scriptures, Warren taught them many practical things including how to outline, preach, give invitations, and lead congregational singing. They put these training sessions into use by preaching in front of the class and receiving his critique. Later a special Preacher Boys night was held in the evening service and each were given a few minutes to preach.

The wives of these future preachers met with me at the same time their husbands were learning about church leadership. We discussed subjects relating to the do's and don'ts of ministry and backing our husbands as God's chosen vessel. Since most of them were young mothers, they were encouraged to make time in their busy schedules to read their Bibles each day, faithfully attend church, and participate in the visitation program.

For a couple of nights, I stayed in the nursery so that the wives could join their husbands in the soul-winning clinic he held. Practicing and presenting the gospel to each other was always followed with actual door-to-door soul winning in an English-speaking neighborhood. Many from the classes became zealous soul winners.

One particular preacher boy, a young Airman, Danny McKittrick, listened well, jumped in, and learned many functions of the church. He led the games in the Friday night AWANA program, directed Patch the Pirate Club, helped instigate a Singles Club, served as church treasurer, assisted in the New Members Class fellowships, and the radio station, participated in our Vacation Bible School, led singing, won many souls, brought visitors to church, and tried to explain to me how to take better pictures. Our home became Danny's home away from the base, and he became special to us, just like a third son. We laughed together, shared meals, and he spent many hours picking Warren's brain with intelligent biblical and ministry related questions.

After my husband died, a man came to me and said, "I feel cheated."

"What are you talking about?" I asked.

"Your husband told me he would teach me how to lead someone to the Lord, and I was going to witness to my Dad when I go back to the States, but he didn't get to do it."

Overhearing what he said, Danny replied, "That's no problem, I can teach you that."

Danny married one of our talented Japanese ladies, Haruna. They moved to the States and after his tour of duty ended, he enrolled in Bible College. While there, he ministered in his local church and gained experience working with people and growing as a Christian and a young preacher. As time passed, he felt the Lord calling him into the military ministry.

He applied to the same mission board we had served with, and met many pastors and made new friends as he and his family traveled from one side of the United States to the other.

Haruna, gifted in art and design, used her talents to create several things for their ministry, including banners, tracts, and websites.

Danny and Haruna have assumed the pastorate of Yokota Baptist Church where my husband invested seven years of his life. They and their three lively boys and one sweet girl will be an asset in their military ministry and in the burden the Lord has also placed on their heart to start Japanese churches.

So, as retired Lt. Commander Todd suggested, Warren's life has come full circle since he reproduced himself.

Now dear readers, you too know...the Rest of the Story!

Reproduce Yourself

"Thou therefore, my son, be strong in the grace that is in Christ Jesus. And the things that thou hast heard of me among many witnesses, the same commit thou to faithful men, who shall be able to teach others also"
(2 Tim. 2:1-2).

Reflect on These Questions

CHAPTER 23 QUESTIONS

Legacy

I feel sure you and your husband left a wonderful legacy too. Take time to tell your story so that future generations might realize their heritage.

1. What would you like for them to know first of all about you?

2. How would you describe your husband for your grandchildren? Of course he was handsome, so do mention his hair, eyes, etc. but also his character traits as: generous, kind, never met a stranger, loved helping others, a fix-it man, etc.

3. Give some examples of things he did (e.g. gardening, mechanical, cooking):

4. List his accomplishments and any special awards he received (military, a doctorate, etc.) or whatever might apply to your special man.

5. If he started his own business, tell when and where. If any of your children followed in his footsteps share it.

Consider

"The steps of a good man are ordered by the LORD: and he delighteth in his way" (Ps. 37:23).

Additional comprehensive questions are provided in chapter twenty-three of:

A Companion Journal,
Good Grief—I Need Relief! A Widow's Guide to Recovering and Rejoicing.

PARTING THOUGHTS FROM MY HEART TO YOURS

$\mathcal{P}$ulling thoughts from my journals for this book proved a mini emotional roller coaster ride, but it allowed me to revisit joy-filled moments as well as sad, painful experiences. I can see through the misty days of grief God's comforting love and guiding wisdom as He sent people to encourage and meet my needs. He will do the same for you, dear widowed friend.

Have you allowed Him to enter the door of your heart? If not, He remains knocking, waiting for entrance, but He won't force His way in. Won't you accept His love gift of eternal salvation?

1. Acknowledge you are a sinner—"For all have sinned, and come short of the glory of God" (Rom. 3:23).
2. Believe that Jesus died for your sin debt—"For the wages of sin is death; but the gift of God is eternal life through Jesus Christ our Lord" (Rom. 6:23).
3. Confess the Lord Jesus as your Savior—"That if thou shalt confess with thy mouth the Lord Jesus, and shalt believe in thine heart that God hath raised him from the dead, thou shalt be saved. For with the heart man

believeth unto righteousness; and with the mouth confession is made unto salvation" (Rom. 10:9-10).

4. Call upon Him to save you—"For whosoever shall call upon the name of the Lord shall be saved" (Rom. 10:13).

If you do this as a result of reading this book, please let me know so we can rejoice together.

Through the guidance of His Word, and the footprint experiences of other widows mentioned in this book, I can say, "I rejoice through my grief journey." I pray and trust the same thing will happen for you as you begin your fresh grief journey or revisit an older one.

May our footprints lead others to Him.

BLESSINGS:

The Lord bless your future, dear widowed friend, be it a life of singleness, a ministry, or a new husband. "The Lord shall bless thee...all the days of thy life" (Ps. 128:5).

Praise Him

"Be thou exalted, O God, above the heavens: and thy glory above all the earth" (Ps. 108:5).

For further encouragement you are invited to join a closed Facebook group called, *The Widow's Zone.*

If you received a blessing from this book, would you please encourage other widows to receive the same by leaving a review on Amazon?

NOTES

i. Taken from *My Utmost for His Highest®* by Oswald Chambers, edited by James Reimann, © 1992 by Oswald Chambers Publications Assn., Ltd., and used by permission of Discovery House Publishers, Grand Rapids, MI 49501. All rights reserved.

ii. Permission granted by Ferree Hardy to use the *Top Ten Tips for Widows*. She is the author of *Postcards from the Widows' Path* (2012). www.widowschristianplace.com.

iii. Dr. Tim Greene, editor, *Baptist Bread Daily Bible Devotions*. (Westland, Michigan 2014).

iv. Raymond R. Mitsch and Lynn Brookside, *Grieving the Loss of Someone You Love: Daily Meditations to Help You through the Grieving Process* (Ventura: Regal Books, 1993) p. 133. Dr. Ray Mitsch granted permission to use the late Lynn Brookside's devotional. www.drmitsch.com.

v. Taken from *My Utmost for His Highest®* by Oswald Chambers, edited by James Reimann, © 1992 by Oswald Chambers Publications Assn., Ltd., and used by permission of Discovery House Publishers, Grand Rapids MI 49501. All rights reserved.

INDEX

ABOUT JOYCE WEBSTER

Joyce Webster, a widowed missionary, retired teacher, published writer, speaker, and mother, coordinates the Grief Outreach ministry at the church she attends, Riverview Baptist Church in Pasco, Washington. Joyce was married to her childhood sweetheart Warren for forty-six years before he died instantly of a major heart attack in Tokyo, Japan. She enjoys working with widows and encourages women to rejoice in the Lord through her weekly radio devotionals, *Rejoicing with Joyce*. She is the founder and president of *Rejoicing with Joyce International*, a non-profit corporation. Connect with Joyce at www.facebook.com/joyce.webster.961, or listen to her devotional radio broadcasts at www.rejoicewithjoyce.org.

A Companion Journal To

Good Grief—
I Need Relief!

A Widow's Guide to Recovering and Rejoicing

Joyce Webster